CONTEMPLATING WITH MEDIEVAL PHILOSOPHERS

Loyev Books

# CONTEMPLATING WITH MEDIEVAL PHILOSOPHERS

by
# Ran Lahav

**Design and Drawings by Karin Fechner**

Loyev Books
Hardwick, Vermont, USA
https://dphilo.org/books

This is Volume 2 of the series *Contemplating with Philosophers of the Past*:
Volume 1: Contemplating with Ancient Philosophers
Volume 2: Contemplating with Medieval Philosophers

Text Copyright © 2024 by Ran Lahav
Drawings Copyright © 2024 by Karin Fechner
All Rights Reserved

ISBN-13: 978-1-947515-28-4

Loyev Books
1165 Hopkins Hill Rd., Hardwick, Vermont 05843, USA
https://dphilo.org/books

# Contents

| | |
|---|---|
| Introduction: Dialoguing with medieval philosophers | 1 |
| Part A: THE EARLY MIDDLE AGES | 3 |
| Chapter 1: Augustine of Hippo | 5 |
| Chapter 2: John Scotus Eriugena | 13 |
| Part B: THE HIGH MIDDLE AGES | 20 |
| Chapter 3: Anselm of Canterbury | 22 |
| Chapter 4: Peter Abelard | 29 |
| Chapter 5: Thomas Aquinas | 37 |
| Chapter 6: William of Ockham | 44 |
| Chapter 7: Nicholas of Cusa | 51 |
| Part C: THE RENAISSANCE | 59 |
| Chapter 8: Marsilio Ficino | 61 |
| Chapter 9: Pico della Mirandola | 68 |
| Chapter 10: Judah Leon Abravanel | 73 |
| Chapter 11: Desiderus Erasmus | 81 |
| Chapter 12: Tullia d'Aragona | 88 |
| Chapter 13: Michel de Montaigne | 95 |
| Chapter 14: Francis Bacon | 103 |
| NOTES | 109 |

*INTRODUCTION*

# Dialoguing with medieval philosophers

This book is about medieval philosophy, but it is not a mere history book. Its purpose is to invite readers to dialogue, personally and creatively, with some representative ideas of medieval philosophers. Thus, the medieval ideas presented here are meant to serve as seeds for reflection about life-issues in general, and about the way they relate to us personally.

This is the second book in this series, after the first which was titled *Contemplating with ancient philosophy*. It is customary to divide the history of Western philosophy into three main eras: ancient philosophy, medieval philosophy, and modern philosophy, which means that the present book is about the second of those three historical periods.

The story of Western philosophy began in the sixth century BC in ancient Greece. This was also the beginning of so-called ancient philosophy, which flourished for about a millennium until the fifth century AD, first in the Greek world and later in the Hellenistic and Roman empires. Ancient philosophers were interested in understanding life and reality in a systematic and rational way, and for this purpose they constructed theories and devised arguments to support them. However, they used philosophy not only for abstract speculations, but also as a guide for living and as a way of life.

Towards the end of the ancient world, Christianity rose to power in the Western world and started influencing people's ways of thinking, and introducing new ideas about life and the world. The result was a new kind of philosophy, which is nowadays called medieval philosophy, or philosophy of the Middle Ages.

Medieval philosophy lasted for more than a thousand years until the sixteenth or seventeenth century, when new ideas gave rise to so-called modern philosophy. As can be expected from such a long era, medieval philosophy is not one thing. It saw developments over time and the birth of a variety of different approaches. We will follow a common distinction and divide it into three main periods: philosophy of the Early Middle Ages, philosophy of the High Middle Ages, and philosophy of the Renaissance.

The last of these three, the Renaissance, was quite different from the earlier two, and some historians regard it as a separate historical period. Here, however, we will adhere to the more common classification of the history of philosophy and regard it as part of medieval philosophy.

## The selection of texts

Most of the philosophers discussed in this book have written about a wide variety of topics, and each of them developed several theories about various issues. We cannot cover here everything written by any one philosopher. This book is not intended to offer a comprehensive history of ideas, but to serve as a brief introduction to medieval philosophy, to give a taste of medieval thought, and to use some selected ideas as material for personal self-reflection. Therefore, each chapter is devoted to one selected idea as discussed by one single thinker. To contemporary readers, medieval philosophy often seems strange and remote, and if this book manages to help readers find meaning and personal relevance in selected medieval ideas, then it will have succeeded in its purpose.

## PART A

# THE EARLY MIDDLE AGES

When medieval philosophy first appeared in the West, around the fifth century AD, Western philosophy was already more than a thousand years old. But the new kind of philosophy was quite different from its ancient predecessor, because it contained new ideas and concerns that had been recently introduced by Christianity, a new religion which started gaining dominance in Western culture. The transition to this new kind of philosophy was facilitated by an event that shook the Western world: In the year 476 AD, the Western Roman Empire fell to German tribes. This event is often seen as marking the end of the ancient world and the beginning of a new world order, that of the Middle Ages or the medieval period, which lasted for more than ten centuries.

Medieval philosophy inherited some important ideas from ancient philosophy, especially from the writings of Plato and Aristotle, but it was also considerably different. God occupied a central place in the medieval world, together with religious notions such as faith, sin and salvation. Philosophical thinking was no longer as free as it had been during ancient times, because it now had to adjust itself to the religious dogmas of the Church. New issues came to the fore, such as the relationship between faith and reason and the place of humankind in God's world.

This new kind of philosophy produced, over the centuries, a rich variety of approaches, a process which can be subdivided into several historical periods. We will start with the

Early Middle Ages, also called the Dark Ages, which lasted from the fifth century AD until about the year 1000. This was a period of cultural decline, with very few institutions of learning and research. Knowledge was preserved primarily in monasteries, while new creative thinking appeared only rarely for short periods of time, thanks to rulers who sought to glorify their courts through the development of culture.

Two thinkers have been selected to represent in Part A the early Middle Ages: Augustine and Eriugena. The first was undoubtedly the most prominent thinker of this historical period, and his influence on Christian thought continues today. The second, while less influential, was almost a lone philosophical light in the cultural slumber of the last centuries of the dark ages. Both wrote about a variety of important philosophical topics, and the specific ideas selected here – Augustine's light of truth and Eriugena's five modes of existence – are representative of their broader approaches.

## Chapter 1

# Augustine of Hippo

## The Light of Truth

### Introduction

Augustine of Hippo (354—430 AD) is commonly regarded as the first major medieval thinker, although he lived in the transitional period between the ancient and medieval periods. He was a philosopher and theologian, a Catholic saint, and one of the most important Fathers of the Church. He exerted a deep and lasting influence on medieval thought and on the Catholic worldview in general.

Augustine was born in North Africa (then part of the Roman Empire) to a pagan father and a Christian mother, and in his youth searched for the truth in Manicheism (a Persian dualistic religion) and Stoic philosophy, until converting to Christianity in his early 30s. Since the Christianity of his time did not yet have a clear theoretical basis, he grappled with fundamental issues at the meeting point between philosophy and theology.

Augustine's way of combining philosophy and Christianity came to serve as a model for many later medieval thinkers. He did not reject "pagan" (non-Christian) wisdom, but acknowledged its important contributions – provided they are consistent with Christian faith.

Faith for Augustine has priority over reason because divine truths cannot be discovered by reasoning alone and must come from divine revelation, as recorded by Biblical prophets and saints, Fathers of the Church, etc., and then passed on to us through tradition. The holy scriptures and the Church are the first and foremost sources of truth, and all reasoning should be accommodated to them. Furthermore, only through faith can we fully understand the truth. Reason without faith is not enough to give us a full understanding. This means that the way to truth passes through religious conversion.

Overall, Augustine's general approach to philosophy had a major impact on later Christian philosophers. In effect, he showed them how Christian philosophy is possible.

## Reflecting: How can I recognize the truth?

For a Christian believer like Augustine, our ability to know the truth is very important. After all, if you want your religion to be based on true knowledge, not just on arbitrary speculations or subjective feelings, you must explain what knowledge is and how it can be attained. The issue is, Augustine says, that even if I encounter a true idea (a truth about God, for example, or about moral behavior), how can I recognize it as a truth?

Augustine assumes, like many other philosophers, that for true knowledge you must experience the truth directly. Thus, you can legitimately say that you know that salt is white or that honey is sweet if you have actually experienced it. But what about abstract or spiritual knowledge which is not based on sensory perception? How can I recognize the moral truth that killing is wrong or that jealousy is a vice, or the religious truth that God is one? These are not truths which I can see or taste or touch.

It would not help to respond that I learned these truths from my teachers, because that would only raise the question how my teachers learned these truths, and how I know that what they told me is true. Neither would it do to respond that I accept these truths on the basis of feelings or intuition, because this would make truth a subjective matter that changes from person to person and would not be a truth at all.

What, then, can reliably tell me that a given idea is true?

## Augustine's Response: The light of truth

Augustine notes that in the material world, the light of the sun enables us to see what is physically true. Without the sunlight you cannot know that, for instance, a tree or a house is standing in front of you. In an analogous manner, he tells us, you need a spiritual light to recognize spiritual truths – to recognize what is morally right, what is justice, what God demands of you, etc. Without the light, you may have all kinds of ideas in your mind, but you would not know which of them is true.

Notice that Augustine is not saying that the light of truth gives you new information, but rather that it makes the truth recognizable to you. You cannot know that your thought is true unless this light tells you: "That's it, you have reached the answer!"

For Augustine, this light is, of course, God. God enlightens us to see that certain beliefs are true. But for the purpose of this discussion, you may think about the light of truth more broadly, to include any kind of abstract truths, whether religious or non-religious.

Augustine's view is called the Doctrine of (divine) Illumination. Some later Christian thinkers supported it, while others criticized it.

*Some **key concepts** to reflect upon:*

- Light
- Truth
- Divine illumination
- Recognition

## Contemplating

For Augustine, although divine illumination is in principle available to everybody, not everybody can use it in their present state. In order to be sensitive to the light of truth, you must first undergo a self-transformation that would make you able to receive it. For Augustine, this transformation is a religious conversion to the Christian faith.

How can self-transformation – whether religious or not – make you sensitive to the light of truth?

Let us try to develop our own personal answer to this question. To do so, our focus will now shift from Augustine's ideas to our own insights. Indeed, as the title of this book suggests, our purpose here is not just to learn what historical thinkers wrote, but also to think *with* them – to think our own thoughts in dialogue with them.

Our main method is contemplating. Contemplation means that we do not just entertain ideas intellectually, and certainly not resort to ready-made opinions, but reflect deeply within ourselves in search of new insights. When we contemplate, we listen inwardly and let new understandings arise in our mind. This can sometimes be accompanied by a sense of marvel, inner silence, and preciousness.

## 1. Text-contemplation

The following excerpts are from Book 4 of Augustine's book *Confessions*, written in Latin between the years 397-400. Read these passages slowly and attentively, savor the words, the images, the ideas. See if the contemplative reading gives you new insights about the light of truth: [1]

> *Errors and false opinions defile the conversation, if the reasonable soul itself is corrupted, as it was in me, when I did not know that it must be enlightened by another light so that it could participate in truth, because the soul itself does not have the nature of truth. You shall light my candle, O Lord my God, you shall enlighten my darkness!*
>
> ...
>
> *And I delighted in these books, but I did not know from where came all that was true or certain in them. For I had my back to the light, and my face to the things enlightened, so that my face, with which I looked at the things enlightened, itself was not enlightened.*

## 2. Visual contemplation

A drawing can evoke associations and understandings that are different from those of verbal thinking. Scan the drawing in this chapter slowly and attentively, gently examine its different elements, and try to comprehend what they tell you about the light of truth. It is best to maintain inner silence and avoid verbalizing your insights prematurely, before they are fully formed. Your insights may be about the idea of light in general, or about specific personal experiences which you remember from the past.

## 3. Issue-contemplation

As we have seen, Augustine offers a religious account of the light of truth. However, isn't it possible to have an experience of recognizing the truth which does not necessarily involve religious faith? What does your own experience tell you about the sense of truth – spiritual truth, moral truth, a truth about life, etc.? Can you characterize it in a way that is broader than Augustine's religious theory, and does not necessarily require religious conversion?

*Seeds of contemplation*

To contemplate on this question, we can use a seed of contemplation – a metaphor or concept to serve as a starting point. Here are several suggestions which you might want to use:

**a)** The image of **night vision**: When I search for a spiritual truth, at first I am like a person searching in the dark who can see nothing. I need "night vision" to see. And just as our physical eyes need time to get used to seeing in the darkness, my spiritual sensitivities too need time to start recognizing spiritual truths. Thus, when I start contemplating on a spiritual issue, I must immerse myself in the darkness of unknowing and wait for a long time until the darkness lifts and the light starts appearing.

**b)** The image of **a clearing in the forest**: The light of truth, like physical light, is blocked by any solid object. Light has no power to push its way through anything; it shines only where there is an opening. Therefore, the light of truth cannot penetrate my mind when I am cluttered with beliefs and assumptions. To receive it I must clear an empty space in my mind, like a clearing in the forest. Only then will rays of light reach me from time to time.

**c)** The concept of **an enlightened teacher**: As long as I am not enlightened, I have no access to the light of truth even when it shines in front of my eyes. But another person who is already enlightened can help me develop my sensitivity to the light. This does not mean that the teacher gives me ready-made truths, but rather helps me develop my own sensitivity to find truths by myself.

# Chapter 2

# JOHN SCOTUS ERIUGENA

## What Does it Mean to Be?

### Introduction

After the fall of Rome, towards the end of the fifth century, Europe sank into a period of cultural decay which lasted until after the year 1000. During those centuries, called the Dark Ages, there was virtually no new philosophy, with one main exception: a short period between the late eighth and early ninth centuries, at the court of Charlemagne (Charles the Great) and his successors. This was the so-called Carolingian period. The most creative philosopher of that period was Eriugena.

John Scotus Eriugena (about 800–877) was an Irish monk and thinker, regarded as the most important philosopher of the Dark Ages. He was invited to the Carolingian court, and as one of the few in Europe who could read Greek, had direct access to books of ancient philosophy. He composed influential translations of ancient texts into Latin and wrote several important books, deeply influenced by Neo-Platonic ideas, most importantly *On the Division of Nature*. This is a large systematic book which presents an overall vision of everything in reality, or in nature as he calls it.

In this chapter we will focus on one important idea in this book: the meaning of existence (being). Notice how Christian concepts (God, angels, saints, sin) are an integral part of Eriugena's worldview, something that characterizes medieval thinking in general.

## Reflecting: Is existence one thing?

Many things seem to exist in reality: stones and trees and human beings, colors and shapes, pains and pleasures and thoughts, numbers, words and sentences, concepts and ideas, time and change, and (according to Christian thinking) angels and God. They are all part of our world; in other words, they exist.

But do they all exist in the same way? Your house exists as an object located in a certain place for everybody to touch and see, but does your joy or anger exist in the same way? Does your finger exist in the same sense that the number five exists, or that the color red exists, or the theory of quantum mechanics, or God and his angels?

Once we start thinking about the many kinds of things that populate our world, we may come to suspect that existence, or being, is not one thing. There may be various kinds of existence that are very different from each other.

So what is existence, and what does it mean to exist?

## Eriugena's Response: Five modes of being

Influenced by the ancient Neo-Platonic thinkers, Eriugena argues that some kinds of existence are higher than others. Some things have a higher being (or existence), so that reality is organized in a hierarchy of being. However, unlike these earlier thinkers, he holds that there is not one single hierarchy, but rather five hierarchies, or more precisely modes of being.

According to Eriugena's first mode of being, something exists when it can be grasped by the senses and the intellect. In this sense, God does not exist, because he transcends our senses and our understanding. He is too high to be existent!

According to the second mode, there is no existence in general, only existence on a specific level in the hierarchy of nature. Thus, if humans exist, they have a human kind of existence, with a body and mind and spirit etc. But angels do not have that kind of existence, so they do not exist. Conversely, if angels exist, then humans do not exist.

According to the third mode of being, actual things have a higher existence than potential things. An example is a real tree versus the potential tree which is contained in a seed.

In the fourth mode, in line with Platonic thinking, ideas are higher than material things. For example, the idea of a triangle exists, while a physical triangle made of three wooden sticks does not exist. This is because the first is perfect and timeless, while the second is approximate and temporary.

The fifth mode of being applies only to humans: Saints exist because they have divine grace, while sinners, who are distant from the divine, do not exist.

Some *key concepts* to reflect upon:

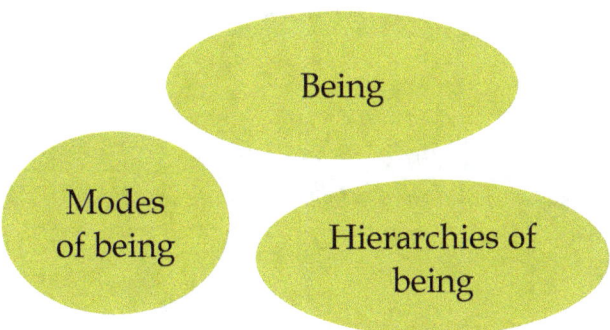

## Contemplating

Beyond the specific details of Eriugena's scheme, his basic idea is both original and deep: Being (existence) and nothingness are not one thing, but rather have different modes. A thing may exist in one mode but not in another. Furthermore, a thing can be non-existent either because it is too high to fit into some level of existence, or too low.

This way of understanding existence seems very different from our normal way of thinking. If it is to be more than a mere play of words, then how can we apply it to our everyday life? Can we translate Eriugena's theory of five modes of existence to the world of ordinary experience?

### *1. Text-contemplation*

Eriugena wrote his text about the five modes of being as a dialogue between master and student. The master tells the student that there are various ways of interpreting the "primordial distinction" between being and non-being, in other words between things that exist and those that do not exist. Then he goes on to explain each one of them.

The passage below is about the second mode of being. Read it slowly, savor the words and notice whether they arouse in your mind new insights about the existence (or being) of things and people in your life:[2]

> *Let there be a second mode of being and not being, which is a hierarchy of natures and creatures ... that begins with the highest angel, and goes down to the lowest functions of the soul, I mean the nourishing and active powers that are involved in the nourishment and growth of the body. ...*

> *The affirmation of the superior is the negation of the inferior, and the negation of the higher will be the affirmation of the lower. Thus, the affirmation of man is the negation of the angel, and the negation of man is the affirmation of the angel, and vice versa. ... Therefore, all the rational and intellectual creatures in the hierarchy can be said both to be and not to be.*

## 2. Visual contemplation

Examine the drawing found in this chapter, silently observe its different elements, and reflect on what they tell you about the hierarchy of being. Be attentive to unexpected insights.

## 3. Issue-contemplation

Eriugena explains how something can have a high level of being in one sense but not in another sense. Can this scheme also apply to your own world of experience? Are there aspects of your life which have for you a greater degree of being (existence, reality) than others? And if so, how significant is this difference?

### Seeds of contemplation

To contemplate on this question, it is useful to start with a seed of contemplation – a metaphor or concept to stimulate our thinking. Here are several suggestions:

**a)** The concept of **vivid presence**: Many routine moments in my life are dull, automatic and thoughtless, and they lack vivid presence in my awareness. In this sense, these moments do not have full being or existence for me. One might even say that in moments of self-forgetfulness or distraction I myself do not fully exist, or that when I act as an automaton I do not exist as a person.

**b)** The concept of **making a difference**: Many things in my world make no significant difference to my life. When I go to the supermarket, whether the background music is this song or that song, and whether I buy for lunch a sandwich or a tortilla – this is not likely to impact anything significant. Such things are replaceable and they do not make a difference to who I am or to the quality of my life. In this sense, they have little or no existence for me.

**c)** The metaphor of **existing for somebody else**: I am not a solitary atom in the world but a member of the human community. If I write a poem that nobody else reads, then the poem has virtually no existence. What I do has existence only to the extent that others are aware of it, or at least are impacted by it directly or indirectly.

*PART B*

# THE HIGH MIDDLE AGES

The Dark Ages, a period of cultural slumber in Europe, lasted from the fifth to the tenth century, interrupted only by brief periods of artistic and scholarly activity. Then, in the eleventh century, Europe started experiencing a cultural awakening. This was a time of creativity, of interest in learning and the arts, of technological developments and social change.

This development took place gradually, with notable ups and downs, with periods of war, famine and plague. From the perspective of the history of philosophy, especially interesting was the twelfth century, which was a time of cultural and social renewal called "The Renaissance of the twelfth century." Universities were founded (the first already at the end of the eleventh century, in Bologna in 1088), ancient Greek classics were translated and made available to European scholars, the arts and sciences flourished, and creative philosophical scholarship and learning appeared across Europe.

An important kind of philosophy flourished in this historical context: scholasticism. Scholasticism was a style of philosophizing which emphasized highly structured reasoning and debates, often involving careful commentaries on classical texts, both religious and philosophical. Although not all the thinkers of that period were scholastic to an equal degree, most of the following chapters offer a taste of this kind of philosophy.

Five prominent philosophers were selected to represent, in the following five chapters, this historical period. Each of them wrote about a broad range of philosophical topics, and the specific ideas chosen here from their writings are intended to be both representative of their thought and relevant to our personal concerns today. Anselm's so-called ontological proof for the existence of God is still being discussed by contemporary philosophers of religion. Abelard's "conceptualist" approach is a reminder of the so-called "problem of universals" which occupied many minds in that period of time. Thomas Aquinas, by far the most influential thinker of the five, wrote about virtually every philosophical issue of the day, but his conception of free will was selected here to represent his general approach to human reality. Ockham is remembered today for his methodological principle famously known as "Ockham razor," but a more concrete topic was chosen for the chapter about him, namely his theory of the language of thought. Finally, Nicholas of Cusa was selected for his famous quasi-mystical theory of Learned Ignorance.

# Chapter 3

# Anselm of Canterbury

## God and Perfection

### Introduction

Anselm of Canterbury (1033–1109), or Saint Anselm, was an Italian philosopher, abbot, Catholic saint, and in the last years of his life Archbishop of Canterbury in England. Nowadays he is best known for his argument for the existence of God.

Anselm was one of the first philosophers after the end of the Dark Ages. In his writings he used rational philosophical thinking to explicate religious concepts such as the divine attributes, sin, and grace. For him, as for Augustine five centuries earlier, faith comes first, and reason serves to clarify and explain it.

One task which Anselm took upon himself was to develop a rational argument proving that God exists. This was not in order to determine whether God exists – for him, the existence of God is already determined by faith – but rather in order to enrich faith. After a long, frustrating period of thinking and searching, the proof suddenly appeared in his mind to his great delight.

Several previous Western philosophers had already attempted to prove God's existence, and their main arguments were given names: The cosmological argument, The argument from design, etc.

The argument developed by Anselm is called "The ontological argument." (Ontological means related to existence.) It was discussed intensively by later thinkers, criticized by many, and modified in an attempt to improve it.

### Reflecting: Can we prove that God exists?

For many religious believers, belief in God does not come from a rational proof, but from non-rational sources such as inner conviction, deep personal experiences, trust in the tradition or in religious authority. Nevertheless, we may still wonder: Is it possible for rational thought to prove that God exists? Such a proof, if successful, would show that it is irrational not to believe in God.

But let us think what we might expect from such a proof. We cannot expect pure reason to prove every detail in the Holy Scriptures. Certainly, no abstract reasoning will show that, for example, God appeared to Moses on Mount Sinai, or that Jesus was crucified on a hill outside Jerusalem. What such a proof might show – if successful – is at most that there exists a perfect being, all-powerful and benevolent. And this would not yet distinguish between the Christian God, Jewish God, Moslem God, and other Gods.

And indeed, for a long time Anselm searched for a rational proof for the existence of God. As he wrote in the preface to his book *Proslogion*:[3]

*I began to ask myself whether there might be found a single argument which... by itself alone would suffice to demonstrate that God truly exists... Although I often and earnestly directed my thought to this end, sometimes what I sought seemed to be just within my reach, while at other times it wholly evaded my mental vision, so that at last in despair I was about to give it up as something which could not be found.*

## Anselm's response: Perfection implies existence

Eventually, after much effort, Anslem experienced an insight from which he formulated his famous argument for the existence of God.

At the heart of Anselm's argument is this idea: The fact that we can think about God as a perfect being proves that he exists in reality. This is because a perfect being, by definition, cannot lack anything, and therefore cannot lack existence. Thus, if God exists as an idea of perfection in our mind, he must also have existence in reality.

This conclusion might seem surprising. After all, you might say, ideas are just ideas. For example, the fact that we can have in mind the idea of dragons doesn't prove that dragons exist in reality. Why, then, should the idea of God necessitate the existence of God?

Because, replies Anselm, the idea of God is special. It is the idea of an absolutely perfect being – or more precisely, the greatest conceivable being: It is impossible to conceive of anything greater than him. Thus, when we have in our mind the idea of God, in effect we have in mind the idea of the greatest conceivable being. And the greatest conceivable being must have everything, including existence. A God who lacked existence would not be the greatest – he would be less than an existing God. So if God exists as an idea, he must exist in reality too.

Anselm's argument has been disputed by many thinkers and defended by others. The discussion still continues today.

## Some *key concepts* to reflect upon:

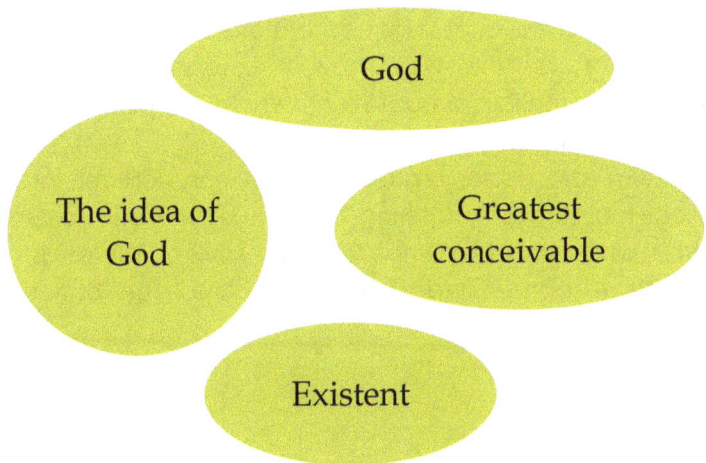

## Contemplating

Anselm's argument assumes that we are able to have in our mind the idea of God as a perfect being. The point is that when we think about him, we are not just uttering the words "God is perfect" but really understanding what we are saying. This is the first step of Anselm's argument, and it is a crucial step. If, contrary to his argument, we are not able to have in our mind the idea that God is perfect, then the argument as whole would fail.

For the sake of contemplation, let us focus on this assumption. Certainly, not everything we can say in words is also thinkable. For instance, we cannot truly think of a square circle, and we cannot truly think that 1+1=7. We can say the words "a square circle" but we cannot conceive what it would mean because it is a logical impossibility.

Is the idea of God as a perfect being (or the greatest possible being) thinkable, as Anselm insists? If so, then how come many people who seem to understand what "God" means deny his existence? Or, as Anselm puts it, how can the Bible say "The fool said in his heart: There is no God"? (Psalm 14:1) (Note, by the way, how philosophical ideas are combined with Biblical quotations, which is characteristic of medieval philosophy.)

Anselm, of course, argues that the non-believer, or the Biblical fool, are only uttering the words "There is no God" without understanding what they are saying. But let us put Anselm's response aside, and delve into the notion of perfection.

## 1. *Text-contemplation*

The following text is from Chapter 4 of Anselm's *Proslogium*.[4] Read it slowly, paying a special attention to the notions of existence and of thinking. What insights can you gain about the thinkable and the unthinkable?

> *No one who understands what God is can conceive that God does not exist, although he can say these words in his heart... For, God is the being which nothing greater than it can be conceived. And anybody who fully understands this, certainly understands that this being exists in such a way, that even in thought it cannot be non-existent. Therefore, anybody who understands that God exists in such a way, cannot conceive that he does not exist.*

## 2. *Issue-contemplation*

The idea of perfection can be found in many cultures in the form of God, The One, nirvana, Buddha, heaven, and so on. Whether we are talking about a perfect god or a perfect human being or a perfect state of mind, the idea of perfection has inspired millions of people, re-oriented their lives, and served as a fountain of spiritual creativity. Even those who do not believe in God often yearn for perfection – they dream of the perfect society, of perfect love, or of becoming perfect human beings.

Putting aside the issue of the existence of God, let us focus on the notion perfection itself: How come we, as imperfect beings, have the idea of perfection, even though most of us have never experienced it? And what role and significance can it have in our lives?

*Seeds of contemplation*

To contemplate on this question, let us use a seed of contemplation – a metaphor or concept to serve as a starting point. Here are several suggestions:

**a)** The idea of **an ideal to aspire to**: Perfection may be an illusion, because most of us have never encountered it in reality. Even so, the idea of perfection plays an important role in our lives: It motivates us to aim high and make an effort to improve ourselves and our society.

**b)** The concept of **hopeful nostalgia**: Although our life is normally very imperfect, in rare moments we experience a glimpse of perfection. At such moments we feel that everything is precisely as it should be, harmonious and perfect. Later – perhaps weeks or months or years later, we may remember these moments with nostalgia and longing. This nostalgia allows us to feel distant echoes of that marvelous experience, giving us hope and optimism.

**c)** The metaphor of **a vague image**: Although we never experience perfection, our ordinary experiences sometimes offer us a vague image of it. This is like seeing something through dirty eye-glasses or through a curtain: You can see that something is moving over there, even though you cannot recognize what it is and what it looks like. Similarly, the experience of perfection allows us to realize that perfection exists, even without experiencing it fully. This vague image of perfection gives us a standard against which we can measure ourselves and our behavior.

# Chapter 4

# PETER ABELARD

## Do Universals Exist?

### Introduction

Peter Abelard (1079-1142) was a French philosopher, logician, theologian, and poet. He is famous in popular culture for his tragic love affair with his student Héloïse. When she became pregnant, her family had him castrated, and he retired to a monastery near Paris and forced Héloïse to become a nun. Their love letters to each other are a literary gem.

As a monk, Abelard continued writing and teaching about a variety of topics, including metaphysics, logic, ethics, and theology. He made major contributions in these fields and became a well-known thinker, teacher and debater.

One of the areas in which he made a significant contribution was the issue of universals, a hotly debated issue in medieval philosophy. A "universal" is a class or type of things such as the class of all dogs, as opposed to an individual dog. The debate was about what sort of thing a universal is. The thinkers of that time offered various answers to this question, mostly extreme views that suffered from serious difficulties. The theory developed by Abelard, called *Conceptualism*, can be seen as lying midway between two extremes.

## Reflecting: Do universals exist?

Imagine that a friend tells you: "Max is my dog." The name "Max" obviously refers to an individual animal that exists in the world: the one owned by your friend. But what does the word "dog" refer to?

This is the famous "Issue of universals" that occupied many minds in medieval times. A "universal" is a general term that designates a type of things, such as species or genera. Examples are the species of dogs (or dogness, so to speak), the kingdom of plants, or the class of all diamonds. What sort of thing is a universal such as dogness, and how does it relate to specific individuals such as the dog Max or the dog Charlie?

At a first glance, you might want to reply: Dogness is something that exists in reality. Reality contains not only individual things (Max, Charlie, John, Mary, etc.) but also types of things (dogs, humans, mammals, etc.). In other words, the universal dogness is something that exists in the objective world.

This response, called "Realism," according to which universals are real things, has been inspired by Plato's philosophy of ideas, but it suffers from serious difficulties. For example, how is the individual dog Max connected to the universal dogness? Are Max and dogness two separate things that exist side by side? We might want to reply that Max "contains" dogness. But does this mean that dogness exists "inside" Max like Russian dolls inside each other? How can one thing turn another thing into a dog? Furthermore, do Charlie and Max contain the same dogness? If so, then how can a thing such as dogness exist in two different places at the same time?

In response to these difficulties, you might opt for an alternative response. You might say that dogness is not a thing in the objective world, but something in our mind: an image or idea or name, which the human mind imposes on things around us. This position, also popular in Medieval times, is called "Nominalism." It holds that universals are mere names. But it, too, suffers from serious problems: If universals are just in our mind or our language, does this mean that the species of dogs does not exist in the objective world and is just an invention of the human mind? If this is the case, then there is a radical gap between our thoughts and objective reality, and this implies that we cannot know much about the world outside us!

Many versions of Realism and Nominalism were developed by medieval thinkers, but all of them suffer from similar problems. So what are universals?

## Abelard's Response: Conceptualism

In response to the problems with Realism and Nominalism, one might want to find a third option, something in between: Universals are not independent things in the world, but neither are they mere inventions of our minds. This was indeed the response of Peter Abelard which came to be known as Conceptualism.

Briefly, Abelard's idea is that universals are concepts which are "abstractions" of objective things. For example, dogness is an abstraction of Max, of Charlie, and of other dogs.

What are abstractions? When our mind examines dogs as dogs, it ignores the differences between them – their different colors, their different heights, etc. – and it focuses on the common element: Their general shape, their four legs, their tails, and so on. Just as you can focus on Max's brown color or on Charlie's black color and ignore the rest, you can also focus on their dogness and ignore the rest.

Thus, dogness is not just a subjective product of our mind – it is based on real facts in the objective world. Yet, dogness is also not an independent thing that exists by itself, like a Platonic idea, in separation from Max and Charlie. It is an aspect of individual dogs.

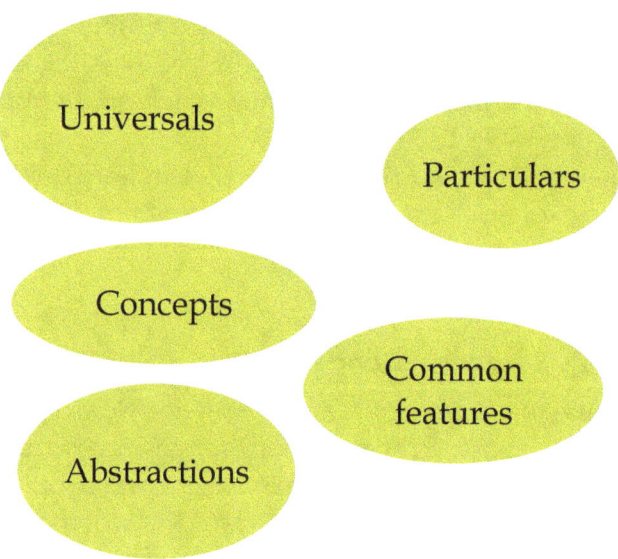

*Some **key concepts** to reflect upon:*

- Universals
- Particulars
- Concepts
- Common features
- Abstractions

## Contemplating

The issue of universals is abstract and remote from our everyday concerns. Let us try to make it more concrete and relevant to our personal lives. One way of doing so is to think about how universals apply to myself.

As a thinking human being, I am aware of myself not just as one human being among many others – in other words, not just as a sample of the general category of human beings, but also as a unique "I." In this sense, I find in myself two facets. On the one hand I belong to the class of all animals, to the class of humans, to the class of males or females, and so on, but at the same time I also understand myself as a unique individual. From my perspective, I am the only person in the entire world who is I.

In short, I am a mixture of universality and unique individuality. How do these two elements interact in my life?

## 1. *Text-contemplation*

To contemplate on this issue, read slowly and attentively the following text by Abelard and see if it arouses in your mind interesting insights about your universality and uniqueness:[5]

> *The conceptions of universals are formed by abstraction... In relation to abstraction, it must be known that matter and form are always mixed together. But the mind's reason has this power, that it may at one time consider matter by itself; it may at another time turn its attention to form alone; and it may then conceive both intermingled.*
>
> *...*
>
> *If a statue is half gold, half silver, I can discern separately the gold and separately the silver which are joined together, examining now the gold by itself and now the silver by itself, thus looking separately upon things which are conjoined, but not looking upon them as if they were really separated. So, too, the understanding considers them separately by abstraction, but does not consider them as separated...*

## 2. *Visual contemplation*

Silently inspect the drawing in this chapter, note its various features, and let it resonate in your mind and suggest to you new understandings.

## 3. Issue contemplation

As noted earlier, in one respect I experience myself as a unique individual, but in another respect I also see myself as having general characteristics, or universals. These two facets of myself interact in my life in complex ways, and at different moments each of them may be more or less prominent in my mind. For example, in the midst of a political debate I may think of myself as a proud citizen of my country, or as a liberal or socialist or conservative, whereas in my birthday party, or in an intimate conversation with my lover, I may feel myself as profoundly unique.

How do these two poles, the individual and the universal, shape my understanding of myself?

*Seeds of contemplation*

We can use a concept or image as a starting point for our contemplation and as a trigger for new insights. Here are several suggestions:

**a)** The idea of **mine but not me**: My experience tells me that I am an individual self who is unique and is like no other person. Admittedly, I have many characteristics which others around me have too – my height, hair color, or taste in food – but these are characteristics that I *have*, not characteristics of who I *am*. They are peripheral to my identity, non-essential aspects of myself. They are mine but not me. Because although the universals (or characteristics) of "human" and "male" and "teacher" etc. apply to me, they do not capture my individuality as I experience it. I am a unique individual who transcends all universals.

**b)** The concept of **uniqueness in freedom**: Often in my life I am a mere human being, defined by general characteristics (or universals) that are shared by many other people. At other times, however, I act out of true creative freedom, and true freedom cannot be captured by general characteristics. When I write a poem, for example, or dialogue heart-to-heart with a friend, my actions – if they are truly free – transcend all pre-existing patterns, all generalizations and laws. At that moment, I am beyond all universals, a unique individual.

**c)** The metaphor of ***Illusory individuality***: From my personal perspective I sometimes feel as if I am beyond all general characteristics or universals. But in fact, this inner feeling is an illusion. In reality I am a human being just like any other. To be sure, I experience myself as unique, but so does every other human being. Even my belief in my pure individuality is a general characteristic, a universal that applies to all humans.

# Chapter 5

# Thomas Aquinas

## What Is Free Will?

### Introduction

Thomas Aquinas (1225-1274) was a major philosopher and theologian of the Middle Ages, one of the greatest thinkers of the Catholic Church, a saint and Doctor of the Church. He and Augustine before him were responsible for formulating much of the philosophical and theological basis of Catholicism.

Thomas Aquinas was born in Italy to a rich and powerful family. After receiving a broad education, he decided to join the Dominican order of the Church, despite fierce resistance from his family which even abducted and imprisoned him. As a Dominican monk he studied in Paris and Cologne, and was called by his fellow students "the dumb ox" because of his big size and his shyness and quietness. Later he started teaching at the University of Paris, and then at several institutions in Italy.

He wrote a vast amount of influential theological and philosophical essays and books on virtually every topic discussed at the time. Among other things, he drew a clear distinction between theology and philosophy, explained the relationship between faith and reason, developed a fuller response to the issue of universals, and reconciled Catholic teachings with the philosophy of Aristotle. His ideas have remained influential in Catholic thinking to the present time.

> Shortly before his death, Aquinas had a deep mystical experience and as a result stopped writing, explaining that all he had written now seemed to him like straw. Soon afterwards, while on his way to the Church Council in Lyon, he fell ill and died.

## Reflecting: what does free will mean?

Imagine that you are at a dinner party, and although you believe in vegetarian principles, you end up eating a big piece of meat pie. Afterwards you wonder: Why did I eat it? Did I do it of my own free will?

Free will is an important philosophical topic for at least two reasons. First, free will is an essential part of how we understand ourselves. We think of ourselves not as automatons, but as capable of choosing freely what to do and how to live. Second, the topic of freedom is closely related to the topic of ethics. You can be morally responsible for your actions only if you did them freely. If you were forced to act and had no choice, you cannot be blamed or praised for what you did.

So what is free will, and what does it mean to act freely?

One might respond that we exercise our free will when we have several options before us and choose one of them. For example, I can either accept the piece of meat pie offered to me, or reject it because of my vegetarian convictions.

But is this a good answer? If I accept the meat pie and eat it, is this necessarily a free choice? Well, it depends. If I eat the pie because the cook forces me with a knife to my throat, or if my boss orders me to eat it and I know that he would ruin me and my family if I displease him, then one may argue that I did not act freely but was forced to eat. Likewise, my eating meat is arguably not a free act if I am distracted and eat the pie without thinking, or if I am starving and have no other food, or if I simply don't know that it contains meat. Even though in some of these cases I "decided" to eat the meat pie, we might say that I did not do so freely.

What, then, is free will?

## Aquinas' response: The freedom to choose the good

Thomas Aquinas follows Aristotle in distinguishing between our will and our intellect. Our *will* is the "appetite" for something we perceive as good, while our *intellect* is our ability to reason or judge. In every choice, says Aquinas, our intellect considers our different options to act and how likely they are to lead us to our goal. But after all the options have been laid out, something else has to choose between them. This is the task of our will, which is free to make the final decision, or so-called "assent."

According to Aquinas, our will always aims at one goal: to achieve what is good, which also includes our own goodness and thus happiness. Even if we choose to steal or hurt ourselves, we do so because this seems to us good in some sense: pleasure, fun, money, power, fame, etc. We cannot choose what does not seem to us good, because our will, by its very nature, wants the highest good.

This implies that not every choice I make is a full expression of my free will, because many choices are not relevant to the good. If, for example, I make a trivial choice between eating an apple or a pear, then this choice is not about the good (being a good person, doing God's will, achieving the highest happiness). Free will is primarily about meaningful choices, such as addressing ethical dilemmas, acting kindly towards others, improving myself, choosing my way of life, spending my time fruitfully, and the like.

Why, then, do we often act in ways that are contrary to the good?

There are several reasons according to Aquinas. Sometimes we confuse the ultimate good with a lower good such as quick pleasure. At other times, we understand the ultimate goal, but fail to realize the proper way to achieve it. We might think, for example, that money will give us much happiness, without realizing that it would bring us only a low kind of pleasure. And still at other times we ignore some of our options because they involve something frightening or repulsive.

Some *key concepts* to reflect upon:

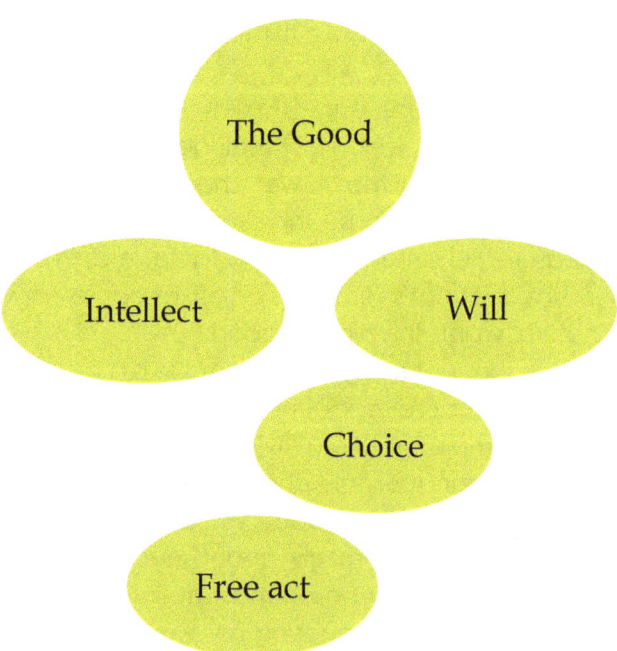

## Contemplating

For Aquinas, as we have seen, we cannot choose the bad freely. This suggests that our capacity to choose freely is intimately connected to our capacity to know the good and the bad. Is this a reasonable view that those two capacities are so closely connected to each other, given our modern understanding of human psychology?

## 1. *Text-contemplation*

Aquinas' great book *Summa Theologica* is built very methodically as a collection of issues, answers, possible objections, replies to the objections, and sometimes additional comments. Here is a fragment from *Question 83: Free Will*, which includes four "articles" (questions or topics), several possible objections, Thomas' own view ("I answer that…"), and his reply to specific objections.

Read the following text attentively and try to discern how it resonates with your personal experience with free choices. To understand his words, remember that for Acquinas, "the cognitive power" is the power to reason, while "the appetitive power" is the power to will or want.[6]

*From Article 3: Whether free-will is an appetitive power*

> *I answer that, the proper act of free-will is choice: for we say that we have a free-will because we can take one thing while refusing another; and this is to choose. Therefore, we must consider the nature of free-will by considering the nature of choice.*

> *Now, two things come together when we make a choice: one on the part of the cognitive power [to reason], and the second on the part of the appetitive power [to will]. On the part of the cognitive power, reasoning is required with which we judge one thing to be preferred to another. And on the part of the appetitive power, it is required that the appetite should accept the conclusion of the reasoning. ...*
>
> *And since the object of the appetite is good in itself, it follows that choice is principally an act of the appetitive power. And thus free-will is an appetitive power*

## 2. Issue-contemplation

Aquinas tells us that free will is a significant ability of human beings because it tends to lead us towards the good. This raises an interesting issue: Doing good is of course important, but why is it important to do so freely, through free will? Isn't it just as valuable to reach the good automatically, by thoughtless habit, or even by compulsion?

To address this issue, look back at your past experience and reflect on how your own free choices have been significant in your life.

*Seeds of contemplation*

To contemplate on this question, we will use a seed of contemplation to orient our thoughts. Here are several suggestions:

**a)** The concept of **achievement**: What is valuable in life is not the good that you happen to possess but the good that you struggle to achieve; not the end result but your path towards it. Now, the path towards achievement requires determination, work and courage. It requires choosing to face your challenges and refusing to quit. This is why to achieve the good you must make choices, in other words use your free will.

**b)** The concept of **creative life-vision**: In order to do good in life we must be motivated by noble aspirations and values. The goodness of our action depends not only on *what* we do but mainly on *why* we do it. Our actions are good to the extent that they are motivated by wise intentions and understandings. We must therefore work to develop a deep vision of life and to act from it. Developing a vision of life is a creative work, and creativity requires making free choices.

**c)** The metaphor of **the lighthouse**: We are all called to do our best in life, and this calling is like a beacon of light in the darkness. But the beacon does not give us precise instructions what to do. Like a lighthouse on the shore, it indicates to us only a general orientation. It is we who must freely decide what to do in order to advance towards the light. Free choice is therefore crucial in the journey towards the good.

## Chapter 6

# WILLIAM OF OCKHAM

## The Language of Thought

### Introduction

William of Ockham (about 1287-1347) was an English philosopher and theologian, and a major thinker of the High Middle Ages. He was born in England, probably in the village of Ockham near London, and as a child was sent to study at a Franciscan house. In his twenties he studied and lectured at Oxford University until he was called to the Papal court in Avignon (in present-day France) because his teachings were suspected of heresy. There he worked on his writings until he became involved in a debate between the Franciscans and the Pope, and escaped with a few fellow Franciscans to Italy and then Germany. In his later years he wrote on political issues, and was excommunicated by the Pope. He died in Munich in 1347.

Ockham wrote about a variety of fields, including logic, ethics, theology, natural philosophy (science), and political philosophy. Overall, in his philosophy he favored a simplified worldview, and his methodological principle called "Ockham's razor" (avoid unnecessary assumptions) is often employed even today.

## Reflecting: In which language do we think?

What happens in your mind when you think? What happens, for example, when you think that the flower in the garden is a rose, or that the red jacket that is hanging on the wall is yours?

Sometimes thinking feels like inner speech. You may be saying to yourself "This is a rose," pronouncing each word silently, inwardly. But more often, you do not feel any inner speech going on in your mind. When, for example, you want to leave the house and you assume that the red jacket on the hanger is yours, you simply take the jacket off the hanger and put it on. If any inner speech goes on in your mind, you are not normally aware of it. Only afterwards, when you find out that you took the wrong jacket, you might say to yourself the words: "Strange, I thought it was mine!" Evidently, when you took the jacket some sort of thinking happened in your head, but not any noticeable inner speech.

How, then, does thinking happen in your mind? Does your mind think in words, perhaps too silent or too quick to notice? And if so, in which language does it think? In your native language or in some special mental language?

A number of ancient and medieval thinkers had commented briefly on this issue before Ockham, but he was among the first to discuss it in detail.

## Ockham's response: Our mental language

Ockham agrees with several previous philosophers that the mind thinks in some sort of language. Thanks to this mental language, the mind can formulate ideas, plan, and reason. However, he argues, mental language, or the language of the mind, is different from the language of speech.

Ockham reasons that the concepts in our mind come from our experience of the world, while spoken words come from cultural conventions. For example, when you think about a dog, your idea of a dog comes from your encounter with dogs. In contrast, when you speak, you use the English word "dog" which comes from the conventional vocabulary of English speakers. Indeed, Spanish-speakers use the word "perro" and French-speakers the word "chien," although all these speakers have in mind the same thing, namely the concept of a dog.

Ockham concludes that our spoken words are different from the language of our thoughts. Although spoken words express the concepts of our thoughts, the two are not the same. The thinking mind thinks not in words but in concepts, which are the ideas behind the words.

Similar considerations suggest to Ockham that mental language and spoken language are different not only in their vocabulary but also in their grammar. The two languages correspond to each other approximately, but the language of thought is more basic, condensed, and logically structured. It expresses the essence of our ideas before speech conventions come into the picture.

Some *key concepts* to reflect upon:

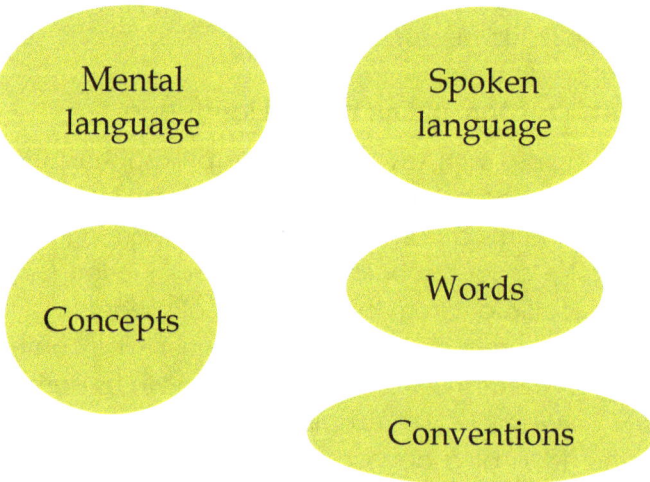

## Contemplating

Consider Ockham's view that our mental language is more precise and logically structured than our spoken language. Is it possible that this picture is reversed, and our mental language is in fact *less* logical and *less* structured than our spoken language, so that our thoughts are more vague or rich than our speech?

One observation in support of this suggestion is that we sometimes feel struggling to express our thoughts in words. We want to articulate our inner understanding, but we feel that it is too nebulous and hazy to put in precise words.

If we take this experience seriously and conclude that our mental language is more vague than spoken language, then we have to explain why this is so. Why can't we always translate the richness of mental language into spoken language? More generally, what do we learn from the difficulty of translating thought into speech?

## *1. Text-contemplation*

To contemplate on the above issue, read slowly the following text by Ockham, reflect on his ideas, and try to understand their meaning, implications, and connection to your personal experiences.[7]

> *I say that vocal words are signs that are subordinated to mental concepts or contents. By this … I mean that words are used in order to signify those things which are signified by mental concepts. Hence, the mental concept signifies something primarily and naturally, while the word signifies the same thing in a secondary way.*

> ... *A concept or mental impression signifies whatever it signifies in a natural way. On the other hand, a spoken or written term signifies something only according to a free convention. From this follows another difference: We can change at will what a spoken or written term signifies, but nobody can change at will the designation of a mental concept.*

## 2. Visual contemplation

Quietly examine the drawing in this chapter and let your mind hover over its shapes and shades. As you do so, try to "listen" to what the images intimate to you.

## 3. Issue-contemplation

What happens within you when you feel bursting with ideas which you are unable to verbalize in spoken words? Why does your speech sometimes seem too crude to verbalize what you understand internally?

### Seeds of contemplation

To contemplate on this question, we could use a seed of contemplation – a metaphor or concept to serve as a starting point. Here are several suggestions:

**a)** The metaphor of **the music of thoughts**: My spoken English consists of a limited vocabulary and a limited number of linguistic structures. In contrast, my inner thoughts are like music which can carry infinite tones of meaning. There is therefore a gap between what my limited speech and what my limitless thoughts can express. As a result, when I try to describe my thoughts in words, I feel like trying to describe a symphony. I am forced to satisfy myself with general, approximate descriptions and ignore the infinite richness of the music of my thoughts.

**b)** The metaphor of ***the pixels of reality***: My inner understandings blend with each other, as well as with my accompanying feelings, creating a myriad shades of meanings. For example, when I listen to somebody's personal story, my understanding of his words is colored by my concern for him, by my impression of his facial expressions, by my hunger or anxiety, and all these mingle with each other and create countless new combinations. In contrast, spoken words divide and separate, each word standing for one standard meaning. In this sense, words act like pixels on a computer screen, which simplify the image into separate points of standard colors. This is why I often feel that my speech is a crude reproduction of my rich inner understandings.

**c)** The concept of ***translation problems***: My deepest thoughts are more like feelings than like conceptual language. They contain pre-linguistic qualities that have been born directly from personal experiences before being shaped into definite words and sentences. Therefore, my inner understanding and my speech speak in two different languages. As a result, in order to describe my understandings in words I must translate one language into another. And as in all translations, not every idea in one language can be accurately translated into the other language.

## Chapter 7

# NICHOLAS OF CUSA

## Learned Ignorance

### Introduction

Nicholas of Cusa (1401-1464), also called Nicholas Cusanus, was a late medieval philosopher and a Catholic cardinal. He was born in Kues (Cusa in Latin) in today's Germany, studied at Heidelberg University and at the University of Padua in Italy, and was made a cardinal in his late forties. Throughout his career he was active in church politics during a period of considerable inner controversies. Nevertheless, he found the time to produce many essays in philosophy, mathematics and theology. He died in Italy at the age of 63 or 64.

Nicholas can be seen as a transitional thinker between the High Middle Ages and the Renaissance. On the one hand, he was influenced by scholastic thinking, a Medieval style of philosophizing involving careful reasoning, debates, and commentaries on classical texts. On the other hand, some of his ideas resonate with later thought. An important theme in his writings is God's relation to the finite world, and thus also the gap between God's infinite reality and our limited human understanding.

One notable example is Nicholas' theory of "*docta ignorantia*" or Learned Ignorance. According to this theory, although we are unable to know God through conceptual reasoning, we can know him through "Ignorance." This is the topic of the present chapter.

## Reflecting: how can I know what is beyond reason?

In several of his essays, Nicholas of Cusa inquires how we humans, with our finite minds, can possibly know God whose reality is infinite and completely transcends our reason.

For Nicholas, God is a coincidence of opposites, in the sense that he includes within himself opposite characteristics: smallness and greatness, highness and lowness, etc. After all, God's infinite reality is the source of everything, including things that are opposite to each other. Therefore, all differences and oppositions coincide in God. This means that God is radically different from a finite object such as a mountain or a house or a human being, which has only certain properties and not others. For example, a mountain has a particular size – it is big but not small, or brown but not blue, while God includes both greatness and smallness, brownness and blueness.

The human mind, which thinks in terms of specific concepts (big, green, animal, bird, etc.) is unable to understand how opposites exist together in the same reality. It is unable to compare God to any other thing, since his "coincidence of opposites" is unlike anything else.

This might seem to imply that God cannot be known at all by humans, except in a negative way, in terms of what God is not. Yet, believers seem to acknowledge God's existence as if they know him. How is this possible?

## Nicholas' response: Knowing through ignorance

Nicholas' response is that although we cannot know God through conceptual reasoning, we can know him through "ignorance." This is not the ignorance of a fool, but the ignorance of somebody who has realized God's transcendence and understood that he is unable to grasp him conceptually. Nicholas calls this state of mind *docta ignorantia* or Learned Ignorance, through which we can know God.

How can ignorance possibly be a form of knowledge?

Nicholas distinguishes between two faculties of the human mind: reason and intellect. Reason understands through concepts. Intellect (in the language of medieval philosophy) is a non-conceptual form of understanding, similar to what we would nowadays call intuitive or holistic understanding. Although we cannot know God through the concepts of reason, we can know him through our Intellect, which means that we cannot verbalize our knowledge in words. The state of "ignorance" somehow involves our "intellectual" knowledge of God.

Nevertheless, God is not completely beyond words. Metaphors and approximations can be used to point to God without describing him accurately. And indeed, throughout his writings Nicholas gives various metaphors that presumably hint at God. He is particularly fond of geometric and mathematic metaphors. For example, like a polygon that can approach a circle but can never become a precise circle, our ideas can approximate God and point to him, yet never capture him. Such metaphors can serve as "signs" or approximations of God, but not more.

*Some **key concepts** to reflect upon:*

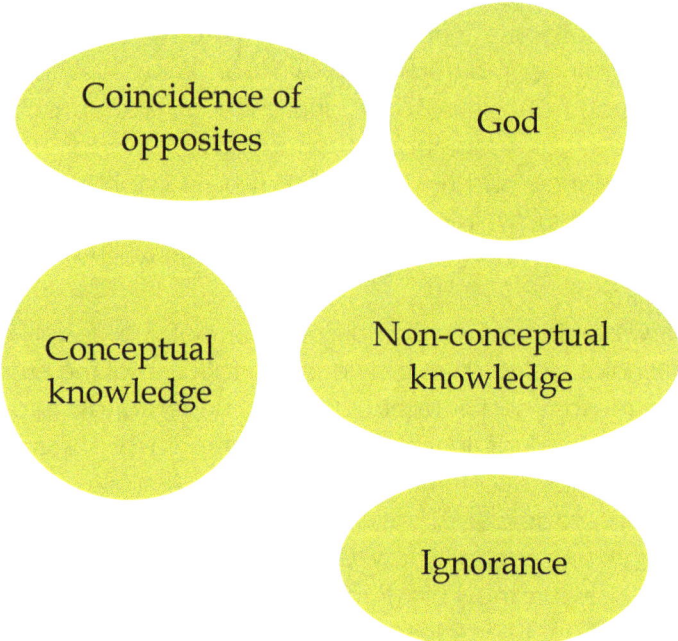

## Contemplating

Nicholas' theory that we can know through ignorance an infinite reality that transcends our finite reason raises perplexing questions. What kind of state of mind is this "ignorance"?

Let us not attempt to understand what precisely Nicholas meant, since that would require a special scholarship of his writings, not to mention a good understanding of Latin, the original language of his texts. Here in this book, we want to use the historical text as a starting point for our own contemplation, and for resonating with its ideas from our own personal experience.

This is, then, our question for contemplation: In your experience, what kind of "ignorant" state of mind can lead you to understand that which lies beyond reason and words?

## 1. Text-contemplation

The following is adapted from Nicholas' essay "The Vision of God." Here he describes how our encounter with God's incomprehensible contradictions can lead us to recognize God as a necessary being, in other words, as an absolute reality that is not dependent on any previous condition.[8]

> *Hence I observe how needful it is for me to enter into the darkness [of understanding], and to admit the coincidence of opposites beyond all grasp of reason, and there to seek the truth where the impossibility [of God's contradictions] meets me.*
>
> *And beyond that, beyond even the highest ascent of the intellect, where I shall attain what is unknown to every intellect, and which every intellect judges to be furthest from the truth, there, my God, are you who are absolute necessity. And the more I recognize that dark impossibility as dark and impossible, the more truly does His necessity shine forth and is more present without veil, and comes nearer [to me].*

## 2. Visual contemplation

Look at the drawing in this chapter, examine it carefully and quietly, and try to discern what its different elements tell you about your personal experiences of knowing through ignorance.

## 3. Issue-contemplation

What happens in your mind when you experience "learned ignorance"? What is it like to have this state of mind?

Some of Nicholas' sentences seem to suggest an experience that is equivalent to mental darkness. Consider his sentence (quoted above): "The more that dark impossibility is recognized ... the more does this necessity shine forth." This implies that the experience of darkness, or ignorance, may have different intensities, sometimes more intense and sometimes less so.

What kind of experience, then, might be involved in knowledge through ignorance?

*Seeds of contemplation*

To address this question, we may use a metaphor or concept as a starting point for our contemplation. Here are several suggestions:

**a)** The metaphor of **a fog of unrealness**: When you walk in a fog, you sometimes get an uncanny feeling that the visible world around you lacks substance. The hazy shapes that appear from time to time through the fog resemble familiar buildings or trees, but their presence feels remote. It is as if they are unreal, like a movie. Yet, through these seemingly unreal shapes, you sense that something real is hidden in the fog. Learned Ignorance may be compared to the experience of objects that are partly hidden in a fog of ignorance.

**b)** The metaphor of **the person behind the face**: When you look at another person, you are sometimes aware of her thoughts and feelings. Strictly speaking, all you can perceive is the shapes and colors of the face, because you can never peek into her inner world. Yet, you sense that a real inner life exists over there behind the face, an inner life that you will never know directly. Learned ignorance might be a similar experience: through the "face" of the world you sense the presence of a hidden infinite reality.

**c)** The image of ***vastness of a landscape***: When you stand on top of a mountain and gaze at the landscape beneath you, you may experience your smallness, as if you are a miniscule creature in a vast reality. You cannot see the details of that greater reality, but its presence somehow arouses your awe and wonder. Words cannot describe that stirring immensity – you fall silent and savor its mysterious presence. Learned Ignorance may likewise involve a sense of awe-inspiring presence that points to an immense reality.

## PART C

# THE RENAISSANCE

The 13th-14th centuries were the high time of "scholasticism," a style of philosophizing which emphasized abstract debates, often related to theological topics. Indeed, the European culture of the time was characterized by a religion-centered worldview which emphasized other-worldly values. But towards the end of the 14th century, a new cultural period emerged in Europe, called the Renaissance ("rebirth"), which showed much interest in the arts and sciences, in human creativity and freedom, and in ancient wisdom.

The Renaissance period followed major destabilizing events, including the Black Death, climate change, famine, and military conflicts, which resulted in new social and political realities. It continued until the rise of Modern Philosophy in the 17th century.

The new spirit of the Renaissance was expressed in many cultural areas – painting, music, literature, science, religion, as well as philosophy. Great thinkers and artists contributed to the new cultural flourishing. The philosophy of the Renaissance was not one thing, but included several different schools of thought, partly overlapping, among them Humanism, Platonism, Aristotelianism, and philosophy of nature. Common to many of them was dissatisfaction with scholastic thinking, and the desire to find new sources of inspiration, especially from the ancient world. Yet, scholasticism was not dead and it continued side by side with other approaches.

It is not easy to select representative thinkers from such a diverse and culturally active period, and moreover, to choose a specific idea from the rich writings of each selected thinker. It is impossible to do justice in this limited framework to the entire range of Renaissance thought. The thinkers that were eventually selected come mostly from the humanist movement, because of its greater interest in human affairs.

Ficino, discussed in the first chapter below, was a prominent philosopher of the early Renaissance, and his discussion of virtue was selected both because of the topic's importance in humanist and Neo-Platonist thought, and its relevance to our everyday life. Pico della Mirandola's famous essay *Oration on the Dignity of Man* is a pillar of Renaissance Humanism. Abravanel and Tulia d'Aragona were both chosen for their discussion of love, a popular topic in the Renaissance, and needless to say, relevant to our lives today. Erasmus, though more famous for his satirical book *The Praise of Folly*, was selected for his discussion of the fragmentation of the mind, which was part of his book on the Christian virtuous life. The selection from Montaigne serves as an antidote to the lofty ideas which Renaissance philosophers often entertained, since it deals with ordinary, everyday life. Finally, Francis Bacon's discussion of the errors of thought represents the rise of scientific thinking during the scientific revolution, which started in the late Renaissance.

# Chapter 8

# MARSILIO FICINO

## IS VIRTUE ONE THING?

### Introduction

Marsilio Ficino (1433-1499) was one of the influential early Renaissance philosophers. He was born near Florence, Italy, spent most of his career under the patronage of the powerful Medici family, and was the tutor of Lorenzo the Magnificent (Lorenzo de' Medici, an important ruler and patron of the arts and sciences). For Ficino, the philosopher's task is to interpret and develop historical treasures of wisdom, since wisdom manifests itself gradually through history. He saw himself as a Platonist, although he also went beyond Plato's doctrines. When Ficino was about 40-years-old, Cosimo de' Medici made him the head of a new Platonic academy, which served to educate the youth and a meeting place for intellectuals. Ficino wrote influential philosophical works, among them translations into Latin of Plato and Plotinus, which became standard translations in Europe for three centuries.

The present chapter relates to Ficino's book *Platonic Theology*, which defends the Platonic ideas that the soul is separate from the body and is higher than material things; that the goal of the soul is to rise and unite with the divine; and that in order to do so the soul must become pure and virtuous.

## Reflecting: What are the components of a virtue?

Imagine that you admire your friend for her moral character, especially her courage and honesty. This means that in your view, courage and honesty are *virtues*.

The concept of "virtue" plays an important role in many historical approaches to ethics which emphasize moral character. A virtue is a character trait which involves a tendency to behave and feel in certain moral ways. A virtuous person is somebody who tends to display virtues.

Which character traits, or tendencies, count as virtues?

There are different approaches to this question. Aristotle, for example, more than a millennium before Ficino, listed nine virtues and divided them into two kinds: ethical virtues such as courage or justice, and intellectual virtues such as wisdom. Marsilio Ficino made a somewhat similar distinction between two groups of virtues: First, ethical virtues, which involve ethical behavior – justice, courage and temperance; second, speculative virtues which involve intellectual clarity – understanding divine things, knowledge of natural things, political prudence, art and skills.

But now, looking at virtues in general, beyond this or that specific virtue, what are the common characteristics of all virtues? What are the components of which any given virtue is made?

This question is relevant to virtue-education. When you educate somebody for some virtue – for courage, for instance, or for honesty – do you teach your student step by step, one component after another? And if so, which component comes first and which comes last?

## Ficino's response: Virtue is indivisible

Ficino's response to this question is found in his major book *Platonic Theology*, where he discusses the nature of virtues as part of his discussion of the soul. According to him, virtues are not made of components, since each virtue is one undivided, holistic quality. Inspired by Plato's *Seventh Letter*, Ficino argues that although the process of ethical training may be long, you eventually acquire the virtue all at once, in a moment of illumination or self-transformation.

Ficino insists that virtues are indivisible because he believes that virtues reside in the soul, which he believes is immaterial and thus indivisible. In any case, his main argument for the indivisibility of virtue is that the idea of a partial virtue does not make sense. If I am honest in one part of my soul but dishonest in another part, or if I am courageous in one part of my soul but a coward in another – this is not virtue, and perhaps is even impossible. To give an example which is not Ficino's, if you steal on some days but not on others, then you are certainly not virtuous. Virtue, then, is a matter of all or nothing. It is one indivisible whole.

Some **key concepts** to reflect upon:

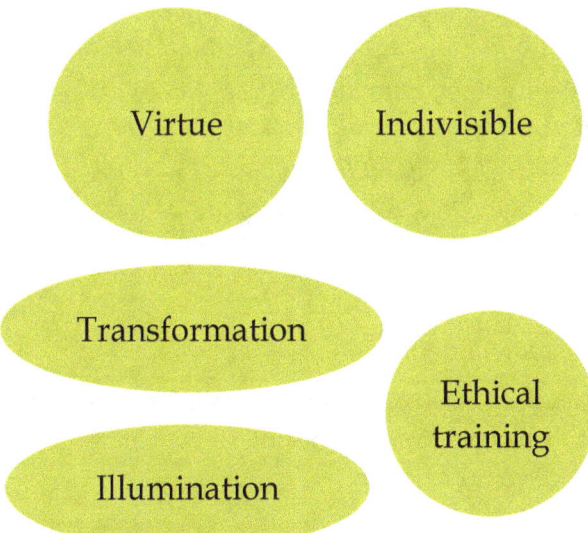

## Contemplating

As we have seen, Ficino believes that you acquire a virtue in a moment of illumination. A deep understanding suddenly fills you and imparts upon you a virtue which you had not had before. Assuming that this is so, what is this illumination and what does it feel like?

### 1. Text-contemplation

Read the following words of Ficino (inspired by Plato's writings), paying special attention to the way he describes the transformative insight. What kind of experience is this, and have you experienced something similar?[9]

> *The light of truth, says Plato, suddenly blazes out in the rational soul, not sparked by things themselves but by a prolonged discussion, like a spark from a stone that is struck many times. Likewise, a young man is disposed to moral behavior through long habituation. As long as some little thing is missing to ignite that unchanging and rational ardor of the appetite [=the will], it is not sufficiently inflamed and he does not yet possess moral virtue. Keep blowing on it, and at last the appetite's flame, sufficient now for virtue, flares up suddenly.*

### 2. Visual contemplation

Examine attentively the drawing in this chapter, and see if it gives you an insight about the nature of Ficino's transformative illumination.

## 3. Issue-contemplation

If Ficino is right and the acquisition of a virtue happens all at once, then this is a dramatic event. One moment you are one kind of person, and the next moment you are transformed into another kind. If so, what exactly happens to you in such a self-transformation?

*Seeds of contemplation*

To contemplate on this question, choose a seed of contemplation as a starting point. Here are several suggestions:

**a)** The metaphor of **the location of a virtue**: When we want to behave according to a virtue which we do not yet possess, we may succeed for a little while, but we lose it once we get tired or distracted. This shows that the virtue is not yet truly ours – it is a mere isolated idea in a corner of our mind. In contrast, a truly acquired virtue resides in our inner center, where it can project to our entire being consistently. Thus, learning a new virtue amounts to a sudden change of location, where the virtue moves from the periphery of our personality to the center of our personality.

**b)** The metaphor of **fountain of inspiration**: What moves us to virtuous behavior is inspiration, since only inspiration can give us the power to overcome our psychological tendency to be selfish, weak-willed and lazy. Without an inner source of inspiration, we could not force ourselves to be courageous, honest, or kind. True virtues appear only when, after much work, the hard rock within us finally succumbs to the pressure and breaks down, letting a fountain of inspiration erupt into us.

**c)** The concept of **understanding my origin**: For a Platonist like Ficino, the goal of my soul is to rise above my material concerns and unite with its origin, which is the highest dimension of reality. But I cannot do so as long as I think that I belong to everyday life and material concerns. In order to rise, my self-understanding must change. I must acquire the deep understanding that I belong to a spiritual order. Now, understanding where you belong is a matter of either-or: either you understand or you don't. That is why the acquisition of virtue, if it happens at all, happens all at once.

## Chapter 9

# Pico della Mirandola

## Human Dignity

### Introduction

Pico della Mirandola (1463–1494) was an Italian philosopher and an influential voice of Humanism, an intellectual movement that believed in the value of human life and potentials. He was born to the Lord of Mirandola, and in his youth studied many branches of knowledge and several languages. He later studied at the University of Padua and the University of Paris. At the age of 23 he composed a list of 900 theses on religion, philosophy and science, and planned to invite scholars from all over Europe to discuss them. This, however, was prohibited by the Pope. At the age of 31 he died of unclear causes, possibly poisoning.

Pico is best known for his short essay *Oration on the Dignity of Man*, which praises the human being for his unique ability to determine his own nature – to rise to the heights of goodness or to sink to shameful existence, depending on his behavior. This unique capacity is a gift from God, who, in the spirit of medieval thought, is at the center of reality. The book is often regarded as a manifesto of Humanism.

## Reflecting: What is special about human nature?

Every creature in our world has a unique nature, or essence. The cat, for example, is a domestic, carnivorous, four-legged mammal that hunts small animals. What about us, human beings? What is our unique nature?

The answer to this question should capture that which is special to humans and which distinguishes us from all other creatures. And indeed, throughout history thinkers proposed a variety of definitions: Man is a political animal according to Aristotle, a mortal rational animal according to the Neo-Platonic thinker Porphyry, the image of God according to Judaism and Christianity, a tool-maker, a speaking animal, and so on.

Pico is not satisfied with an objective, factual definition. He wants a definition that would explain what gives humans their special value and dignity. He wants to explain their central place in the universe – an idea that is in line both with Humanism's emphasis on the value of humans, and with the traditional Christian view that places humans at the center of God's creation.

What, then, are our essential capacities that make us who we are and give us our special value?

## Pico's response: The dignity of self-determination

Pico suggests that free will is what makes humans unique. That in itself is not a new idea, since various earlier thinkers believed that freedom is a unique human capacity. But Pico's response is more radical. For him, you are free not just to act one way rather than another, but to determine what you are. We humans have the gift of self-determination.

This means that our human nature is not fixed, but is something we are free to shape. It is up to each one of us to make our nature low or high, as low as that of beasts or even vegetables, or as high as that of angels, or anything in between.

Our power of self-determination, or in other words the freedom to determine who we are, says Pico, is the source of our unique dignity. Unlike all other creatures, whether animals or angels, which have a fixed location in the hierarchy of being, we have the special privilege of being the only ones who can determine where in the universal hierarchy we would be.

Some *key concepts* to reflect upon:

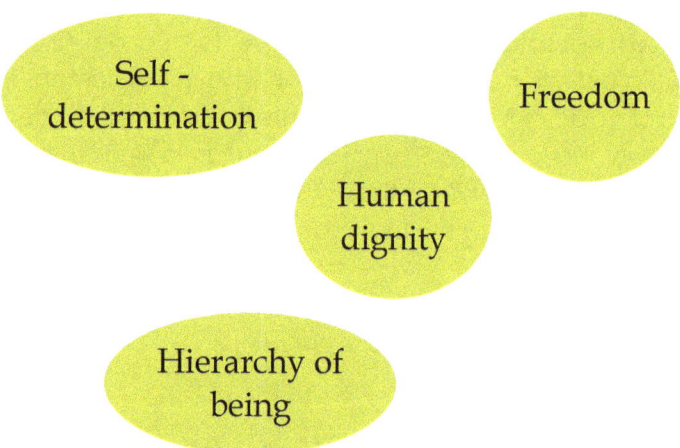

## Contemplating

Pico's philosophy can be said to bring together three important concepts to explain human nature: self-determination (the freedom to determine who you are), the hierarchy of being (a being may be higher or lower than others), and human dignity. To what extent do these three concepts apply to you, or even shape who you are?

## 1. Text-contemplation

Read carefully the following excerpt from *Oration on the Dignity of Man* and see how it might apply to the person you are and to your own personal life.[10]

> *O supreme generosity of God the Father, O highest and most marvelous happiness of man! To him it is granted to have whatever he chooses, to be whatever he wills. ...*
>
> *Whatever seeds each man cultivates will grow to maturity and will bear in him their own fruit. If he is vegetative, he will be like a plant. If sensitive, he will become brutish. If rational, he will grow into a heavenly being. If intellectual, he will be an angel and the son of God. And if, like no other created thing, he withdraws into the center of his own unity, his spirit made one with God in the solitary darkness of God who is set above all things, he shall surpass them all.*
>
> *Who would not admire this chameleon? Or who could admire more greatly any other being?*

## 2. Issue-contemplation

If Pico della Mirandola is right and we humans have the special ability to determine ourselves, then is this necessarily a good thing? Should we rejoice over it or lament it?

*Seeds of contemplation*

To address this question, choose a seed of contemplation as a starting point for your thinking. Here are several suggestions:

**a)** The metaphor of **prisoners of a hierarchy**: If, as Pico tells us, my behavior can raise me or lower me in the hierarchy of being, then this imposes upon me an immense task which I have not chosen. I have been born into this hierarchical world as a human being, and as a result I am now forced to struggle my whole life for my position in it. In this sense I am a prisoner. Animals are more fortunate than me, because they have a fixed nature that was given to them, so they don't have to worry about their place in the hierarchy or be anxious about rising or falling.

**b)** The metaphor of **the art of self-creation**: If I am free to determine my nature, then I am like an artist who creates his own portrait. I am my own artwork. This means that my life is not just a meaningless sequence of events determined by arbitrary factors, because I have the capacity to infuse in it the beauty and meaning of a great work of art.

**c)** The concept of **power**: My ability to determine my own nature gives me an immense sense of power. I am the one to decide which virtues I will possess, which values will guide my actions, and indeed who I am. I am the superpower of my life, and I feel gratified and proud to have such a power.

## Chapter 10

# Judah Leon Abravanel

## The Circle of Love

### Introduction

Judah Leon Abravanel (about 1460-1530) was a Portuguese-Italian Jewish philosopher and poet. He was born in Portugal to an intellectual and influential Jewish family. His father was an important commentator of the Bible and an advisor to the king, but because of political intrigues he had to flee to Spain. In 1492 the Spanish king and queen ordered all the Jews in Spain to convert to Catholicism or go to exile, and the Abravanel family decided to avoid conversion by going to Italy. There, Leon Abravanel associated with important scholars and wrote his main philosophical works.

Abravanel's most famous book is *Dialogues of Love*. Love was an important topic in the philosophy of the Renaissance, and the book gained popularity and influence. The text is structured as three dialogues between two characters: Philo, a male character who represents love, and Sophia, a female character who studies philosophy and represents the search for wisdom.

These names are taken, of course, from the word Philo-Sophia, in other words philosophy, or love of wisdom. Through the dialogues between them, the book discusses the nature and origin of love, addressing a variety of issues such as the relationship between love and desire, love and happiness, and love and beauty.

## Reflecting: Descending love and ascending love

Like many other Renaissance thinkers, Abravanel views love not as a mere subjective emotion, but as a metaphysical power that emerges from a divine source and acts on all levels of reality. The idea that reality (or Being) is organized on several levels, one above the other, was familiar to Renaissance thinkers, and Abravanel envisions it with God at the top, angels underneath him, then humans, animals, material objects, and lastly unorganized matter, or chaos.

Love, Abravanel explains, flows through this universal hierarchy in a "circle of love," from the top to the bottom, and then back to the top again. It originates in God, from there it descends through the levels of Being down to the lowest matter, which is chaos, and from there it ascends again through the levels of Being back to the starting point, to God. Thus, the cosmic circle of love consists of two parts: One half-circle of descending love in which each being loves its inferior that is situated under it, and the second half-circle of ascending love in which each being loves its superior situated above it.

It may seem odd to think of love as a power that flows down and up through the levels of Being. For our purpose, it would be easier to understand the idea of ascending and descending love if we focus on love among human beings. Abravanel observes that we sometimes love somebody who is "higher" than us, while at other times somebody who is "lower" than us, in other words our superior or our inferior. The examples which he gives include the love between parent and child, teacher and student, ruler and citizen, or any two individuals who are unequal in their authority, power, knowledge, etc.

From this perspective, the character Sophia asks the character Philo: How does love ascend from a "lower" person to a "higher" one, or conversely descend from a "higher" person to a "lower" person?

To understand this question, compare your love for a person who is "above" you whom you respect and admire – your parent or teacher or leader, for example – to the love of that person for you. Abravanel asks: Is loving above you and loving below you the same sort of love? Do you love your parent in the same sense that you love your child, or do we need two different definitions of love?

### Abravanel's response: Two kinds of love

Abravanel does not find a satisfactory answer in Plato's famous theory of love. For Plato, to love somebody is to desire to possess what you lack, and thus to bring yourself closer to a state of perfection. The problem is that this does not seem to apply to loving somebody who is below you. A superior person does not lack what an inferior person has. For example, while children lack their parents' wisdom and respect them for it, parents do not lack their children's wisdom and do not yearn to attain it.

Abravanel concludes that love is not always a desire for what you lack. When you love somebody lower than yourself (your student, your child, your follower, etc.), what you desire is to give your beloved what he or she lacks. When parents love their children, they seek not their own perfection but the perfection of their children.

In contrast, the inferior person who loves the superior person desires something else – to unite himself with the superior and in this way to attain his own perfection. Consider, for example, how young children identify with their parents, how they look up to them and often feel proud of them, as if the greatness of the parent was their own. Their love is a love of unification (or identification, as we might say nowadays), unlike the opposite love, of a parent to a child, which is a love of giving or bestowing.

It follows that the love of parents for their children is different from the love of children for their parents. Love is not one thing but two!

## Some *key concepts* to reflect upon:

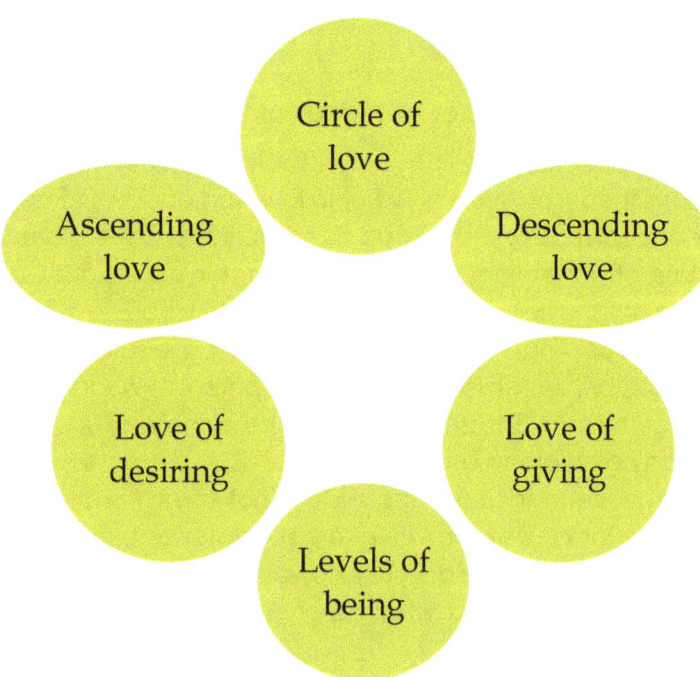

## Contemplating

Most of us have personal experiences that support Abravanel's view about the asymmetric nature of love, suggesting that your love for somebody you adore is usually different from your love for somebody who adores you. Assuming that this is so, why do we call these two kinds of love by the same name – "love"? Is this a linguistic error, or do they nevertheless have something essential in common?

### 1. *Text-contemplation*

Read the following text slowly, savor the words, try to sense their meaning, and see if they can shed light on the issue.[11]

> Philo: *Not less efficacious, but perhaps more efficacious is the love of the father to the son, and of the master to the disciple, and of the cause to the effect, than the love of the inferior to the superior. Because the superior ones do greater things with their love for the inferior ones by making them develop and improve, while the inferiors do nothing except desiring to approach the superiors' perfection.*
>
> *Also, since the inferior ones have no beauty which the superior ones lack and for which they love them, the superior ones would love their own beauty to participate in the inferior, in whom it is lacking. And in this participation the superior ones become more beautiful, since their inferiors are beautified by them, and by the beauty of the whole universe.*

## 2. Visual contemplation

Examine the drawing in this chapter slowly and gently, and let it speak within you. What insights does it give you about the apparent dual nature of love?

## 3. Issue-contemplation

Try to remember cases in which you loved somebody as your superior in authority or knowledge (teacher, parent, boss, etc.) and cases in which you loved somebody as your inferior (your child, student, etc.). What does your experience tell you about the similarities and differences between these two loves? To what extent can you consider them as different versions of one and the same thing?

*Seeds of contemplation*

To contemplate on this question, you may start with a seed of contemplation – a metaphor or concept that can trigger relevant insights. Here are several suggestions:

**a)** The concept of **preciousness**: What is common to both kinds of love is your attraction to somebody you consider precious. Whether you regard the object of your love as inferior or superior to you, whether it is a dog or a king, in all cases you are attracted to their preciousness.

**b)** The metaphor of **the center of your world**: When you love somebody, that person is close to the center of your world, regardless of superiority or inferiority. And the more you love that person, the more prominent that person is at the center of your being. Your decisions and preferences, your emotions, your thoughts and plans – all these come to revolve around your beloved, however much above you or below you he or she is.

**c)** The metaphor of **symbiosis**: The more you love somebody, the less sharp is the boundary between you and your lover. As your love for that person grows, the lover's happiness becomes almost your own happiness, and the lover's suffering your suffering. In extreme cases, you can no longer distinguish between your wishes and the wishes of your lover, as if you possessed them together. Whether that person is inferior to you or superior to you, the two of you are like two organisms who have merged into one.

# Chapter 11

# Desiderius Erasmus

## THE BATTLE FOR VIRTUE

**Introduction**

Desiderius Erasmus (1466-1536) was a Dutch Renaissance thinker and scholar and a Catholic theologian. He was born in Rotterdam, was educated at religious schools, and became a priest in his early twenties. He studied at the University of Paris, then taught at the universities of Cambridge and Oxford and at other universities in Europe. He died in Basel at the age of 69.

Erasmus was an important thinker of Humanism, which (as we saw previously) emphasized the value of human life and potentials. Described as "Prince of the Humanists," he wrote a number of influential essays and translations. During the Protestant Reformation, he sympathized with the criticisms of the Catholic Church, yet chose not to leave it. His most popular book, *In Praise of Folly* (1511), is a satire of the Catholic Church, as well as other sections of European society.

Erasmus' main interest was ethics and the Christian ethical life. He never wrote a grand ethical system, but something close to it is found in his book *Handbook of a Christian Knight*, published in 1501

The book was written in response to a request to compose a guide for those who wish to live according to Christian faith, and it became a popular work. It describes the life of virtue as focused primarily on our inner life, beyond mere external behavior and rituals.

## Reflecting: How to achieve a life of virtue

How can we attain a virtuous life? This is the central issue of Erasmus' *Handbook of a Christian Knight*.

The answer to this question depends in part on how we understand human nature. If, for example, we believe that human nature is naturally good, then we are likely to hold that living spontaneously and freely would bring out the best in us. In contrast, if we assume that humans' natural tendencies are egotistic, then we might contend that virtue must be imposed through discipline and strict training.

As a humanist, Erasmus did not believe that human nature is wholly sinful. On the other hand, like most other Europeans of his period he was a devout Christian, and Christianity believed in the reality of human sinfulness. For him, therefore, both good inclinations and bad inclinations are strong powers in our lives. Given this duality, how should we understand the road to the life of virtue?

## Erasmus' response: Reason as the unifying ruler

Erasmus' book starts with a dramatic warning: "We must be constantly aware of the fact that life here below is best described as being a continual warfare." In other words, living an ethical life is a difficult task that requires constant struggle and vigilance. This is why the book is titled "Handbook of a Christian Knight."

The root of the problem is human nature, as portrayed by Erasmus: We humans are not unified beings. We are fragmented and influenced by conflicting forces, which are of two different kinds: material motivations and spiritual motivations. The former orient us downwards towards material things, as when we are driven by desires for money or for excessive eating and drinking and pleasure. The second kind of motivations orient us upwards, towards spiritual matters. Thus, a human being is fragmented – and here Erasmus adds an instructive metaphor – like a society that is torn between different groups of people with different interests.

The fragmentation of human nature poses a serious problem for the ethical life, because it makes our behavior inconsistent, full of distractions and contradictions. We are also under constant attacks by temptations, which are difficult to distinguish from true spiritual motivations. As a result, we tend to fail in our moral tasks and sink low. The question is how to counteract this fragmentation and restrain the power of negative motivations, so as to nurture the virtuous life.

Erasmus' response is that we humans have a third kind of force, in addition to the material and the spiritual, which can control the other two, impose on them cooperation and orient them upwards. This third force is reason – the human ability to judge correctly and govern over our behavior. Reason, like a king who rules over a fragmented society, can control the various human factions and enforce harmony upon them, so that each of them would perform its specific duty for the good of society.

*Some **key concepts** to reflect upon:*

## Contemplating

We may sympathize with Erasmus' attempt to identify an inner "king" to unify and orient our diverse inner powers, but we may still wonder: Why choose reason as the "king" and not some other function of the soul such as conscience, or faith, or love, or the yearning for truth?

*1. Text-contemplation*

The following excerpts are from the beginning of Erasmus' book *Handbook of a Christian Knight*. Read them slowly, notice the challenges required to achieve virtue, and reflect on the role of reason in these battles.[12]

> *Man is an extraordinary compound of two or three distinct parts: a soul resembling something godly, and a body that is like a brute beast. ...*
>
> *Man may therefore be compared to a divided society, which, being composed of diverse classes of people with different interests and inclinations, is distracted with divisions and commotions, unless there is somebody in the highest authority who is able and willing to work for the good of the whole. And it is necessary that the wisest should rule, and the simplest should obey.*
>
> *... Now, the only king in man is reason. ... And these are the special characteristics of a king: First, he ought to be wise, or else he would err through ignorance; next, he should want to do only what he thinks is right.*

## 2. Visual contemplation

Examine the drawing found in this chapter while reflecting on the ideal of inner unity oriented towards virtue. What insights does the drawing give you about this task, and about the role of reason in your own experiences?

## 3. Issue-contemplation

Erasmus' view that the virtuous life requires a strong unifying inner center – a "king" – raises a question: How exactly should this inner center manage the many elements of your being – your likes and dislikes, your fears and desires and yearnings, your spontaneous urges and your habits?

*Seeds of contemplation*

The following seeds of contemplation might help you as starting points for your reflection.

**a)** The metaphor of **the shepherd**: Many of my conflicting motivations are mostly innocuous, as long as I manage to keep them within appropriate boundaries. Therefore, the role of my inner center is to keep my motivations in their place, like a shepherd tending his sheep. He keeps them in their pen at night, and during the day takes them out to their grazing fields. There he makes sure that they stay where they are supposed to be and do not wander to where they might cause trouble.

**b)** The metaphor of **the company manager**: Most of my inclinations are potentially useful, and when they work in harmony with each other, they can do great things. Even my fears and angers have their role in the whole. I only have to ensure that they all work in coordination with each other towards my overall goals. This is, then, the task of my inner center: to function like a company manager who manages hundreds of workers and makes sure that they all perform their designated roles.

**c)** The metaphor of **the missionary**: Many of my tendencies and urges are too strong or too weak or misdirected, and they are often useless or destructive. I wish they were different from what they are, and some of them can indeed be converted. This is the task of my inner center – to convert my negative energies into positive ones, like a missionary who converts the souls of unbelievers.

# Chapter 12

# Tullia d'Aragona

## THE INFINITY OF LOVE

## Introduction

Tullia d'Aragona (about 1503-1556) was an Italian poet and one of the very few female philosophers of the Renaissance. She was a courtesan, fortunately born during a limited period of time in which courtesans were given relative economic and social freedom. As a child, she was educated in the classical humanities by a cardinal who might have been her biological father, and she demonstrated special intellectual gifts and interests. As a young woman she became successful as a poet and writer, and was in touch with important intellectuals and writers, some of whom were her lovers. She later turned her house into a philosophical academy. Not much is known about her last years, but it appears that her health gradually deteriorated until her death.

Tullia is best known today for her short book *Dialogues on the Infinity of Love* (1547). Philosophy of love was of much interest at the time, and the book became popular. The book mostly contains a dialogue between Tullia and Benedetto Varchi, who in real life was a famous intellectual from Florence, and was also her friend and supporter. The dialogue is probably fictional, although some scholars believe that it may have been based on real conversations.

## Reflecting: Is love infinite?

In her book *Dialogues on the Infinity of Love*, Tullia D'Aragona raises the question whether love is finite or infinite, in other words whether the motivations that animate love are limited to finite durations and circumstances, or whether they can keep animating love endlessly. Through an imaginary dialogue between Tullia and the intellectual Varchi, the book presents several opposing considerations. On the one hand, if loving means the enjoyment of togetherness with your beloved, then there is nothing in the nature of love to prevent it from lasting forever. The joy of being with that person can go on and on and need not ever reach an end. In this sense, love might be "infinite."

On the other hand, if love is a desire for a reachable goal, for example a desire to possess the body of your beloved, then once it attains this goal, it should be satisfied, lose its motivation and die. By analogy, if you desire to break an athletic record or to visit the Taj Mahal, then once you attain this goal, your desire is satisfied and you no longer experience it (although you may now develop a new desire to reach this goal again, or at a higher level). Such a love is "finite" in the sense that by its very nature it is destined to end within a finite period of time once it reaches its goal.

## Tullia's response: Love's goal is impossible

Varchi argues that if love has a definite goal, then it must be satisfiable, which means that it is finite. But Tullia rejects his assumption that a love that has a definite goal must have a reachable end-point. She suggests that although love does indeed have a goal, this is an impossible goal and is therefore never reached.

In order to make this point, she distinguishes between two kinds of love: "vulgar" love in which the lover seeks physical satisfaction, and "honest" or "virtuous" love in which the lover has the impossible desire to merge with the beloved and become one, both in spirit and in body. Clearly, you cannot merge with another person, certainly not physically. Love in this higher sense can continue indefinitely without satisfaction, and it is therefore infinite.

*Some **key concepts** to reflect upon:*

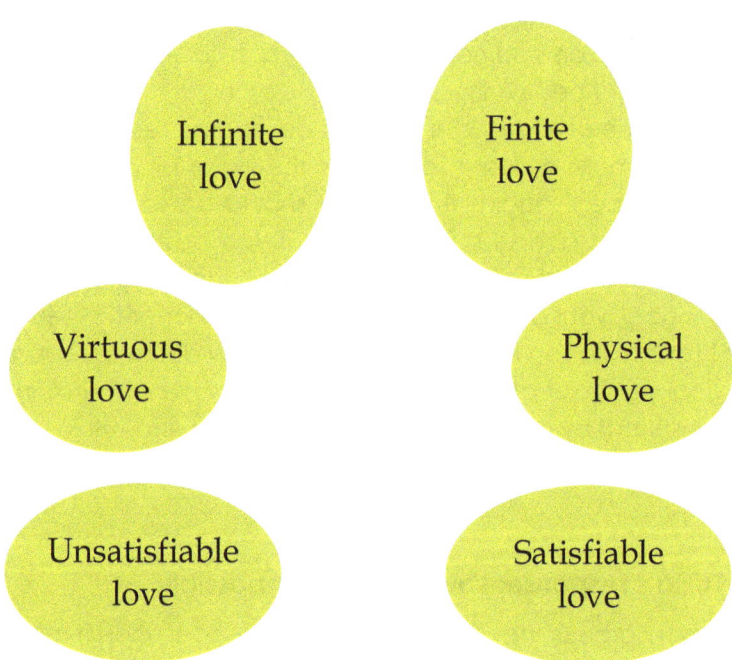

## Contemplating

If Tullia is right, then the word "love" is ambiguous, because it designates two different emotional states: "vulgar" love is a desire for self-satisfaction, while "virtuous" love is a yearning for merging. We may understand intuitively the emotions she has in mind if we consult our own personal experience, as well as novels, movies, or poems. But thinking more precisely, beyond intuitive understanding, how valid is this distinction? Are these really two different kinds of emotion, or two variations of a single emotion? How do they differ from each other in terms of associated feelings, thoughts, behaviors and inclinations?

### *1. Text-contemplation*

The following excerpts are from Tullia's book *Dialogue on the infinity of love*. Read them slowly and attentively, and see if they resonate with your own personal experiences. Try to determine whether your experiences suggest one or two kinds of love, and what their similarities and differences might be.[13]

> *Love is of two kinds: The one we will call "vulgar" or "dishonest," and the other "honest" or "virtuous." Dishonest love appears only in vulgar and rude people, that is, those whose souls are low and vile, and who are without virtue or refinement (whoever they may be, whether their lineage is small or noble). It comes from a desire to enjoy the loved object, and its goal is no other than the goal of brute animals: to obtain pleasure and to generate a creature that resembles themselves, without any further thought or care. Those who are moved by this desire and who love with this kind of love, once they reach what they desire and fulfill their will, will stop their motion and love no more...*

> *Honest love, which is proper to noble people, that is, those with a refined and virtuous soul, whether they are poor or rich, is not generated by desire like the other kind of love, but by reason. Its main goal is to transform oneself into the beloved thing, with a desire that the beloved thing would be transformed into oneself, so that lover and beloved would become one ... And since this cannot be done except spiritually, this kind of love can take place primarily in the spiritual feelings. ... But since the lover also desires a bodily union with the beloved in addition to spiritual union, seeking to be one with the beloved as much as he can, and since he cannot do this because bodies cannot penetrate each other, he can never attain his desire and can never arrive at his goal.*

## 2. Visual contemplation

Quietly inspect the drawing in this chapter and see if any of its details relates to your personal experience of loving. What does this tell you about Tullia's "virtuous" versus "vulgar" kinds of love?

## 3. Issue-contemplation

Tullia argues that "virtuous" love is spiritual in nature. Why spiritual? Why is the desire to merge with your beloved spiritual, and why is it more spiritual than "vulgar" love that seeks self-satisfaction? Indeed, in what sense can a given love count as spiritual or non-spiritual?

*Seeds of contemplation*

The following are "seeds of contemplation" that can serve as starting points for your reflections on the issue:

**a)** The metaphor of **transcending yourself**: Spiritual means seeking to go beyond yourself, especially beyond self-serving tendencies to seek satisfaction for yourself. Only a love that transcends your self-interests can rise beyond the self and take part in the horizons of the spiritual. Thus, a love that is focused on your own satisfaction is not spiritual, while a love that seeks the well-being of others is spiritual.

**b)** The concept of **spirit to spirit**: Spiritual means belonging to the realm of the spirit, which lies beyond sensory qualities such as shapes and tastes and colors. Therefore, a love is spiritual only if it aims at the spirit of the beloved, not at the body or bodily appearance. Such a love is spiritual in the sense that it takes place between one spirit and another spirit.

**c)** The concept of **longing for eternity**: The realm of the spiritual, whatever precisely it is, is infinite. It lies beyond material objects which are finite in size and duration, and which exist in particular places and at particular times. Therefore, a love for an object that exists in space and time, such as a person's body, is a material kind of love. Only love for something eternal, such as a soul or a spirit (assuming that it is eternal), can be spiritual.

## Chapter 13

# Michel de Montaigne

## WHAT AM I?

### Introduction

Michel de Montaigne (1533-1592) was an influential French philosopher of the Renaissance. He was born to a wealthy family in southwest France, where his father, Lord of Montaigne, gave him a rich education at home. He later studied law at the University of Toulouse and then served in various political positions. After his father's death he became Lord of Montaigne. He died of quinsy (abscess in the throat) at the age of 59.

The discussion below deals with his major book *The Essays*, which he revised several times between 1571 and his death. It is written in a personal and conversational style, with many anecdotes, digressions, autobiographical notes, and quotations from ancient writers. Montaigne attempts here to describe human life honestly and truthfully. Unlike many thinkers before him who focused on the "noble" aspects of life, Montaigne pays special attention to concrete human situations and seemingly trivial details, including his own personality flaws and everyday behavior. The result is an unsystematic discussion, often brutally honest, which presents life not as a grand heroic quest, but as a daily struggle with small human weaknesses.

### Reflecting: What is the essential part of me?

When you examine yourself, you find a wide variety of details which make up what is presumably yourself: your body and your desires and fears, your spiritual hopes and your automatic reactions, your ethical ideals and your silly thoughts, your sense of humor and your toilet behavior. All of these seem to be parts or aspects of you.

But are they all equal parts of who you are? Are you simply a collection of all these things?

Normally you do not regard your finger and your political convictions as equal parts of who you are. Even though your finger is part of your body which is part of you, you probably do not regard your finger as representing who you are. After all, while you spend much time expressing and refining your political views, you normally pay little attention to your finger (unless it hurts), and while you might be eager to explain and defend your political opinions at great length, you rarely do so regarding your finger. Evidently, some aspects of yourself seem to you more essential than others to who you are.

And indeed, many thinkers throughout the ages assumed, whether implicitly or explicitly, that some aspect of ourselves is at the core of our being – usually our soul or our mind, our intelligence or our reason, our freedom, our consciousness, etc. These are, presumably, who we truly are. In contrast, it was often assumed that bodily needs and material interests are peripheral to who we are.

So how do you decide what is central to who you are? This question has important implications for our lives. It determines which aspects of ourselves we want to cultivate and develop, or conversely treat thoughtlessly. It determines where we want to invest our efforts and hopes, which part of ourselves we can be proud or ashamed of, and how we assess our life and the lives of others. It also influences many of our smaller decisions: Shall I spend the evening watching a comedy on television, or doing physical exercises to develop my muscles, or reading philosophy?

## Montaigne's response: I am all of me

Montaigne scoffs at our tendency to identify ourselves with the "noble" parts of ourselves and neglect the "lower" parts. For him, my "lower" bodily functions are no less parts of who I am. The tendency to identify ourselves with our "higher" faculties is not based on rational criteria, but on the wishful thinking to see ourselves higher than what we really are. We prefer to forget that we also wipe our noses, have sex, and visit the toilet periodically.

Let us not pretend, Montaigne tells us, that we are body-less angels! As he says: "I am a man, nothing human is foreign to me." And also: "Kings and philosophers shit, and so do ladies."

This does not mean that we should pay equal attention to every aspect of our lives and cultivate our cleaning habits just like our university studies, or devote ourselves to drinking just as much as to philosophical conversations. It means, rather, that we should acknowledge all aspects of life as legitimate parts of who we are and give each one of them its proper place in our lives.

Here Montaigne goes against some religious and philosophical thinkers who despised the body and the desire for fun and pleasure. He believes that we should accept our physical and psychological needs and enjoy the small pleasures of life, though without becoming enslaved to them.

## Some *key concepts* to reflect upon:

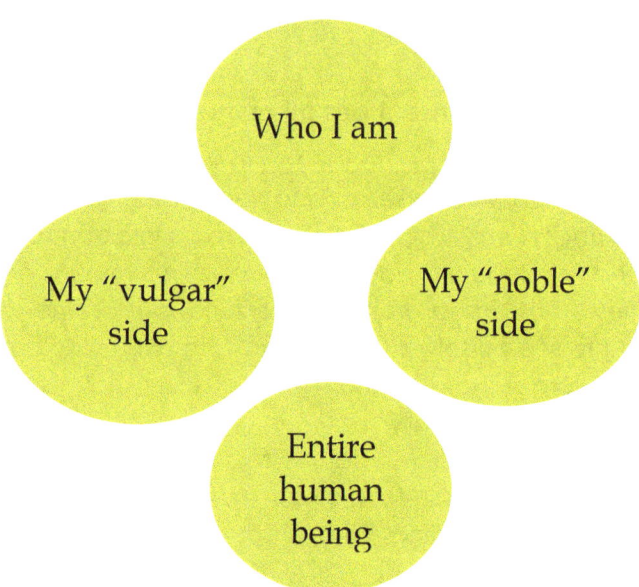

### Contemplation

Which aspects of yourself – your body, your talents, your beliefs or values, your habits, your personality, and so on – do you regard as the most significant or valuable part of who you are? Similarly, which aspects of your friends and acquaintances do you regard as most significant or valuable? And importantly, what are the reasons on which you base your answer?

### 1. *Text-contemplation*

In the text below, Montaigne objects to our tendency to identify ourselves with our "higher" qualities and to exhibit them in public, and he criticizes those who strive to transcend bodily needs and pleasures. What kind of life would you lead if you agreed with Montaigne's statements? Let this question hover in your mind as you read slowly the following excerpts from his book *Essays*.[14]

> *People want to put themselves outside themselves and escape their humanness. It is a folly: Instead of transforming themselves into angels, they transform themselves into beasts; instead of elevating themselves, they pull themselves lower. These transcendental absurdities frighten me, as do high and inaccessible cliffs and precipices. ...*
>
> *It is an absolute and, as it were, divine perfection for a person to know how to loyally enjoy his being. We seek other qualities because we do not understand how to use our own, and we go out of ourselves because we do not know how to reside there. It doesn't help to stand upon stilts, because even upon stilts we must still walk with our legs. And when seated upon the most elevated throne in the world, we are still seated upon our bottom. The most beautiful lives, in my opinion, are those which follow the common and human model, without miracle and without extravagance.*

*2. Visual contemplation*

Look at the drawing found in this chapter, examine its details slowly and gently, and see what insights it might trigger in your mind.

## 3. Issue-contemplation

Let us reflect on our issue carefully, and try to respond to it with good, solid reasons. So which aspects of your life are more central to who you are, and what are your reasons for saying so?

*Seeds of contemplation*

Here are some suggested seeds of contemplation to serve as starting points for your reflections.

**a)** The concept of **self-improvement**: I will adopt the following principle: I am entitled to regard a certain area of my life as essential to my identity when I can improve myself in that area. If, for example, I like swimming, and if my body has good physical potentials, then I might invest myself in swimming and regard this as an important part of my identity and life. And if I succeed in competitions, I will earn the right to feel proud of my achievements. In contrast, it is silly to feel proud of what I received without effort, such as the money I inherited from my parents, or my beautiful hair.

**b)** The concept of **moral character**: The most significant part of me, which determines the value of my life, is my ability to make myself a better person. For instance, if working to develop my taste in wine is not likely to make me a better person, then my wine-tasting abilities are peripheral to who I am. In contrast, if my sense of justice can make me a better person, then it is essential to my being.

**c)** The concept of **sources of happiness**: We all seek happiness, and this suggests that happiness is something central to our lives. Therefore, that which makes no difference to my happiness, or at least to the happiness of people around me, is not an important part of my identity. For example, my smartness is important in my life if it helps to make me or others happy, while the color of my hair may be irrelevant to my happiness and thus not essential to who I am. This is why my wisdom and maturity are so central to who I am, because they contribute greatly to my happiness in all circumstances.

## Chapter 14

# Francis Bacon

## THE IDOLS OF THINKING

### Introduction

Francis Bacon (1561-1626) was an English philosopher, nobleman and politician of the late Renaissance. He is known for his contribution to the scientific revolution of his time, which produced the first discoveries of modern science.

Bacon was born shortly after the death of the astronomer Copernicus, was a contemporary of the astronomers Galileo and Kepler, and died a few years before the birth of the physicists Boyle and Newton. But although these and other scientists were making important strides, a clear understanding of the scientific methodology was missing. He therefore worked to formulate methodological guidelines for science, inspired by the idea that scientific research should consist of careful observations and experimentation as a basis for theories about nature. Although his specific scientific ideas did not prove fruitful, his quest for a rigorous experimental method inspired others and made him one of the fathers of modern scientific thought.

The following discussion deals with Bacon's major book *Novum Organum*, published in 1620. The title refers to Aristotle's book *Organon* that deals with logic. Thus, Bacon's title means: A new system of logic.

## Reflecting: How does our mind distort the truth?

Modern science started to emerge in the fifteen and sixteen centuries, when scientists were beginning to conduct systematic investigations of natural phenomena, and Bacon tried to develop principles that could help guide their research. He had little patience for the scholastic discussions of the Middle Ages, which imposed abstract concepts on the world. Serious research, he believed, must be based on careful empirical observations, because only by observing nature – not just by thinking about it in your armchair – can you develop fruitful theories about the general laws that govern the universe.

The idea of constructing theories on the basis of empirical observations is fundamental to modern science, and for us today it might seem obvious. But is it really obvious?

Imagine yourself at a time before the birth of modern science – what exactly are you going to observe? Are you going to stare at stones and trees and clouds? If, for example, you see a leaf falling to the ground, or a cloud floating in the sky, what will you conclude? How are you going to conceptualize what you observe and translate it into a general theory? The same applies to laboratory experiments: If you decide to bake a yellow round stone in an oven and observe the result, what will you conclude if the stone darkened and splintered into three fragments?

These simple examples suggest that without prior understanding, it is very difficult to know what to observe and how to interpret what you observe. It is no wonder that many thinkers at the time ridiculed Bacon's idea.

Bacon searched for a fruitful way to think about scientific observations and hypotheses. As a first step, he reasoned, we should understand how *not* to think, in other words how to avoid thinking errors. If we can get rid of our thinking biases and distortions, then we can hope to launch serious scientific research and truly learn about nature.

The question thus arises: What are people's main thinking errors? Which tendencies of our mind should we be careful to avoid in order to improve our scientific investigations?

### Bacon's answer: The four "idols"

Bacon called our thinking errors "Idols," and he divided them into four kinds:

First, the "idols of the tribe": These are general human tendencies that can distort objective judgement. An example might be our tendency to pay more attention to colorful objects than to what is hidden from our eyes.

Second, the "idols of the cave," which are thinking errors that are peculiar to the individual. Here we let our judgement be influenced by our particular personality, our education, our life experience, etc.

Third, the "idols of the market," which result from everyday language, which is often inaccurate, ambiguous, and vague.

Fourth, the "idols of the theater," which result from the influence of past philosophers, for example Neo-Platonic thinkers who tried to impose spiritual ideas on nature.

*Some **key concepts** to reflect upon:*

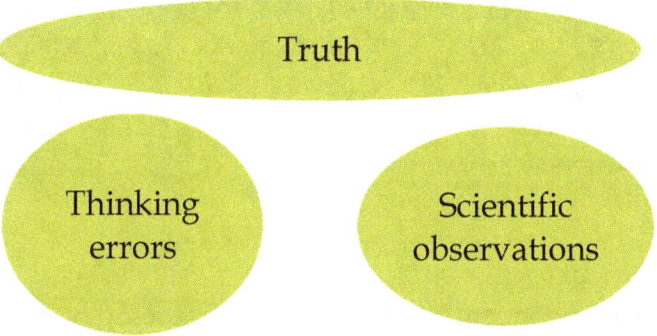

## Contemplation

If we want to work towards avoiding the "idols" that distort our thinking, as Bacon suggests, then a good first step would be developing a fuller awareness of how they arise in our minds. What does your experience tell you about the states of mind that create thinking distortions in your thinking, and conversely, those states of mind that minimize them?

### *1. Text-contemplation*

In the following excerpts from his *Novum Organum*, Bacon discusses some of our human tendencies, or "idols of the tribe," that distort our understanding. To what extent do you find these distorting tendencies in your own mind, and how do they influence you?[15]

> *The human understanding does not resemble a pure light, but is infused with desires and emotions, which generate their own ideas, because man always believes more readily that which he prefers to believe. He therefore rejects difficulties – because of his impatience to investigate; sober thinking – because it limits his hope; the depths of nature – because of superstition; the light of experience – because in his arrogance and pride he does not want to appear preoccupied with trivial and transitory matters; paradoxes – because of his fear of common opinions. In short, his feelings mix with, and corrupt his understanding in innumerable and sometimes imperceptible ways.*

### *3. Issue-contemplation*

Bacon's concern with thinking errors is focused primarily on scientific thinking, but for the sake of our contemplation let us broaden the scope of the discussion to also include distortions in moral judgments, wishful thinking in political thinking, thinking errors in business and work relations, family life, understanding ourselves, understanding others, and in short, in everyday life in general. To what extent should we be guided by the concern to avoid errors?

The two extreme answers seem problematic. If we are always afraid of possible mistakes and do everything in our power to avoid making them, then we are likely to be paralyzed and never reach any decision. If, conversely, we are careless about the possibility of errors, then we are likely to find ourselves naïve victims of irrational fantasies.

What, then, is the proper balance between the two extremes?

*Seeds of contemplation*

The following are suggestions for seeds of contemplation that can serve as starting points for reflection.

**a)** The concept of **defensive skepticism**: It is better to be careful than a gullible fool, and I take upon myself the challenge to defend myself from all potential errors. I will adopt a distrustful attitude to life, suspect any idea I encounter as potentially false, and check it again and again until I am completely convinced that its truth is free from any shadow of doubt. As a result, many of the ideas accepted by ordinary people will be a "maybe" for me. This will make me a skeptical person who possesses only few beliefs, but my sense of confidence will be worth it.

**b)** The concept of **delving into experience**: I don't want to be a victim of false opinions, but I also don't want to be an obsessive skeptic. I want to live my life fully. Therefore, to the extent possible I will free myself from all opinions and speculation, and devote myself to experiencing life. I will delve into what I can see, hear, sense, enjoy, and will have little interest in anything that goes beyond my direct experience. In this way, my world will become narrower, with few opinions and speculations, but also safer from errors and richer with experiences.

**c)** The image of **the anthropologist's viewpoint**: Theories and opinions are enriching and intellectually stimulating, and I don't want to given them up. But I will entertain them carefully, only as ideas and not as truths. I will continue to read and think about ideas – scientific, political, religious, psychological, personal – but as merely interesting, not as true. The truth or falsity of opinions will not interest me anymore. I will look at life as if I was an uninvolved anthropologist observing from the outside a foreign tribe: fascinated by their ways of thinking, but not taking sides on what is right and what is wrong.

**NOTES**

For the sake of ease of contemplation, many quotations in this book have been slightly edited, especially to modernize old-style choice of words and sentence-structure. In addition, some fragment numbers have been changed to agree with the numbering commonly used today.

1. From Augustine's Confessions (397-400), Book 4. Adapted from Pusey, Edward B. *The Confessions of Saint Augustine.* New York: Frederick Stokes, 1910, pp. 91-95.

2. From John Scotus Eriugena's *The Division of Nature* (written around 865), Book 4. Adapted and translated from *De Divisione Naturae, libri quinque.* Aschendorff: Monasterii Guestphalorum, 1838, p. 3. (Compare to the English translation in *Periphyseon: The Division of Nature,* translated by I.P. Sheldon-Williams, revised by John O'Meara. Montreal: Editions Bellarmin, 1987, pp. 27-28.)

3. From Anselm of Canterbury's Proslogium (1077-1078), preface. Adapted from *St Anslem: Proslogium, Monologium, An appendix, In behalf of the fool by Gaunilon; and Cur Deus homo.* Translation by Deane, Sidney M. Chicago: Open Court, 1903, pp. 1-2.

4. Ibid., p. 10.

5. From Peter Abelard's *Logica Ingredientibus* ("Logic for beginners," published in 1121). Adapted from McKeon, R. *Selections From Medieval Philosophers, vol. 1. Augustine to Albert the Great.* New York: Charles Scribner's Sons, 1929, pp. 245-247.

6. From Thomas Aquinas' *Summa Theologica,* Question 83: Free Will. Adapted from *The "Summa Theologica" of St. Thomas Aquinas.* Translated by Fathers of the English Dominican Province. London: Burns, Oates & Washburne, 1920, Volume 4, pp.152-153.

7. From William of Ockhams' *Summa of Logic* (1323) I, c, i. Adapted from Boehner, Philotheus. *Ockham: Philosophical Writings.* London: Nelson, 1957, p. 48.

8. From Nicholas of Cusa's *The Vision of God* (1453). Adapted from Runes, Dagobert, *Treasury of Philosophy*. New York: Philosophical Library,1955, p. 298.

9. From Marsilio Ficino's *Platonic Theology* (1482), Chapter 8, Section 3. James Hankins (Editor), translated by Michael J.B. Allen with John Warden. Volume 2. Cambridge, Mass. : Harvard University Press, 2002, p. 289.

10. From Pico della Mirandola's *Oration on the Dignity of Man* (published in 1496). Adopted from Ernst Cassirer, Paul Oskar Kristeller, John Herman Randal. *The Renaissance Philosophy of Man*. Chicago: University of Chicago Press, 1945, p. 225.

11. From Abravanel's *Dialogues of Love* (1535), third dialogue. Translated and adapted by the author from *Leone Ebreo (Giuda Abarbanel), Dialoghi D'amore*. Bari: Gius, Laterza & Figli, 1929, p. 378.

12. Erasmus' *Handbook of a Christian Knight* (1501), Chapter IV: Of the outer and inner man. Adopted from Phillip Wyatt Crowther. *The Christian's manual: compiled from the Enchiridion Militis Christiani of Erasmus*. London: Rivington and Hatchard, 1816, pp. 38-41.

13. From Tullia d'Aragona's *Dialogue on the Infinity of Love* (1547). Translated from the Italian by the author and adopted from Alessandro Zilioi. *Della infinità d'amore dialogo di Tullia D'Aragona*. Milano: G. Daelli, 1864, pp. 61-63.

14. From Michel de Montaigne's *The Essays* (first published in 1580),"On Experience." Adapted from Carew W. Hazlitt. *The Essays of Michel de Montaigne*. New York: Burt, Volume 2, p. 621.

15. From Francis Bacon's *Novum Organum* (1620), section 49. Adapted from Joseph Devey (editor). *Novum Organum by Lord Bacon*. New York: Collier, 1902, p. 26.

www.ingramcontent.com/pod-product-compliance
Lightning Source LLC
Chambersburg PA
CBHW070150080526
44586CB00015B/1930